WJEC CBAC

Foundation Students' Book

GCSE English/English Literature

Roger Lane

OXFORD

UNIVERSITY PRESS

OXFORD
UNIVERSITY PRESS

Great Clarendon Street, Oxford OX2 6DP

Oxford University Press is a department of the University of Oxford.
It furthers the University's objective of excellence in research,
scholarship, and education by publishing worldwide in

Oxford   New York

Auckland   Cape Town   Dar es Salaam   Hong Kong   Karachi
Kuala Lumpur   Madrid   Melbourne   Mexico City   Nairobi
New Delhi   Shanghai   Taipei   Toronto

With offices in

Argentina   Austria   Brazil   Chile   Czech Republic   France   Greece
Guatemala   Hungary   Italy   Japan   Poland   Portugal   Singapore
South Korea   Switzerland   Thailand   Turkey   Ukraine   Vietnam

Oxford is a registered trade mark of Oxford University Press
in the UK and in certain other countries

British Library Cataloguing in Publication Data

Data available

ISBN-13: 978-0-19-834974-7
ISBN-10: 0-19-834974-2

10 9 8 7 6 5 4 3 2 1

Printed in Italy by Rotolito Lombarda.

Acknowledgements

The publisher would like to thank the following for permission
to reproduce photographs:

P17 Ferruccio/Alamy; **p27** Paul A Souders/Corbis; **p33** Sally
and Richard Greenhill/Corbis; **p41** Esa Hiltula/Alamy; **p45**
Brand X Pictures/OUP; **p65** Bettmann/Corbis; **p66**
Bongarts/Getty Images; **p84** Frank Chmura/ImageState/Alamy;
109 Moviestore; **p115** John Vachon/Corbis; **p119**
Photodisc/OUP; **p123** Philipp Mohr/Alamy; **p127** Galen
Rowell/Peter Arnold,Inc/Alamy; **p130** Graham Lawrence/Alamy
RF; **p131** Najlah Feanney/Corbis Saba;

We are grateful for permission to include the following
copyright material in this book:

Robert Swindells: Extract from *Stone Cold* (Hamish Hamilton,
1993), copyright © Robert Swindells 1993, reprinted by
permission of Penguin Books Ltd.
John Steinbeck Extract from *Of Mice and Men* (Penguin, 2000),
copyright © John Steinbeck 1937, 2000, reprinted by permission
of the publisher.
Roddy Doyle: Extract from *Paddy Clarke Ha Ha Ha* (Secker &
Warburg, 1993), reprinted by permission of The Random House
Group Limited.
Geddes Thomson: 'The New Boy' from *The Other Side of the Clyde*
(Hodder and Stoughton)
Max Schmeling:Extract from 'The Story of a Hero' taken from
www.auschwitz.dk.
Hack Green Secret Nuclear Bunker: Extract from *Hack Green
Secret Nuclear Bunker* Leaflet, reprinted by permission of the
publisher.
Roger Lane: Extract from prize letter, reprinted by permission of
the author.
Kip McGrath Education Centres UK: Extract from English and
Maths leaftet, reprinted by permission of the publisher.
Lorna Smith: Extract from 'The relationship between home and
school' from www.bbc.co.uk.
J B Priestley: Extract from *An Inspector Calls* (Heinemann
Education, 1947), copyright © Estate of J.B Priestley 1947,
reprinted by permission of PFD (www.pfd.co.uk) on behalf of the
Estate of J.B Priestley.
William Marshall: 'Tramp'
Gillian Clarke 'Peregrine Falcone' taken from *Gillian Clarke
Collected Poems* (Carcanet Press, 1997), reprinted by permission of
the publisher.
Dylan Thomas: Extract from 'Extraordinary Little Cough' taken
from *Collected Stories* (Dent, 1983), reprinted by permission of
David Higham Associates Ltd.
Toni Cade Bambara: Extract from 'The Lesson' taken from
Gorilla, My Love (Random House Inc, 1972), copyright Toni Cade
Bambara 1972, reprinted by permission of The Womens Press

Contents

To the student

If you are a Foundation Tier candidate, the chances are that you do not feel particularly good about your English. You may lack confidence and think that you can't read, you can't write and you can't do exams. Well, this book doesn't offer professional psychiatric help, but it does attempt to express in plain English what you can do to help yourself. There are various tasks for you to complete and questions to consider – answers and explanations can be found in the Teacher's Guide which accompanies this book.

Set your sights fairly high. Foundation Tier grades run from G to C, and the book deals with what you need to do to be in and around the C grade. You may be closer than you think to that standard. Think positively and give yourself the best chance – read in detail, write in sentences, learn how to use the full time in the exams. Now it starts...

Roger Lane

Roger Lane

Author's acknowledgement
Thanks to Hugh Lester for his advice and thorough checking, and to Dr Allan Jones and the students of St John's, Newton, Porthcawl for their invaluable help and support. Special thanks to Don Astley, gentleman, scholar and Crewe supporter – WJEC's own Dario Gradi!

Author's dedication
This book is dedicated to the memory of Jack Hetherington, whose wit and wisdom live on and still inspire us.

Unit 0.1

Pen behaving badly?

HANDWRITING

'Handwriting? You don't get marks for handwriting, so what's this all about?'

There are no marks for handwriting, but there are for good presentation and organization, as well as for a general sense of accuracy. There is no recommended style of writing, so you need not lose your identity, but there are commonsense questions to answer:

- Can both the writer and the reader read the writing? (Is it legible?)
- Can the writer write quickly enough? Can the reader read it quickly? (Is it fluent?)

To see how efficient your own handwriting is, answer the following questions honestly. Can you identify any problem features in the way you write?

1. Do you confuse some lower-case letters with upper-case or capital letters? Example:

THE Rain in SPAIN falls mAinly on the Plain

Comment: This could just be a bad habit in someone's writing, so it might take only two minutes to put it right. However, it is worth just checking out that all your letters, upper and lower case, conform to the accepted rules.

2. Do you leave gaps between letters when you write?
Example: *I am a very neat writer, though admittedly rather slow. I believe in spacing out my letters and i can even stretch out further on occasions.*

Comment: This kind of writing may be neat and legible, but it is not fluent, either for the writer or the reader. Joined-up writing is not necessary, but, if you do 'print', make sure that it works efficiently for you and does not slow down the communication.

3. Do you form some of your individual letters badly? Example:

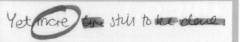

Comment: Fluent for the writer, but a nightmare for anyone trying to read it! The answer to the problem lies in looking at individual letters – Is your o closed at the top? Does your n look any different from your u? etc.

4. Do you write with too few or too many words per line?

Example: I've always written like this and I can't possibly change at this late stage of my life ! By the way, my hobby is shouting!

As for me, I'm very neat and tidy and I'm good for the school budget because I don't use up much paper. In fact, if you want, I will try and get my entire GCSE course on one piece of A4 paper.

Comment: More headaches for teachers and examiners! If you are anywhere near these extremes in your writing, you MUST change your ways. Take the average handwriting as between eight and ten words to a line and you won't be far wrong. If you currently write four or twenty-four words to a line, you are seriously out of order and you should make a significant effort to increase or decrease the size of your writing. It can be done…

5. Are there too many crossings-out when you write?

Example: I ~~was~~ am ~~very quite~~ a little ~~worried~~ concerned about ~~slips~~ errors in my ~~work~~ writing.

Comment: It is good for students to be thoughtful about their choice of words, but, if you think you make too many crossings-out, you do need to take stock of the way you write your sentences. In the example above, the writer would be advised to think of the whole sentence before starting to write it. In this way, the number of crossings-out would be reduced.

6. Does your writing drift across the page, leaving the left-hand side sloping?

Example:
I start off right across on the left hand side of the
page and then slowly slide to the right as if I
am on the deck of a capsized boat. It could
be because I lean my head on my arms
when I am writing…

Comment: This should be easy to correct. Do so now because the habit is preventing you using paragraphs properly.

7. Do you change your style of writing halfway through a piece of work?

Example: I think I shall start writing today with an upright, neat-and-tidy look, but *let's move on to something a little stylish* or even some joined-up mature-looking, fountain pen-type writing. Wait! How about something a little individual and distinctly ME!

Comment: No thanks! It's good fun on a keyboard, but do not experiment in the middle of a serious piece of handwritten work. Keep to your sound, basic style of writing.

You may have other bad habits, such as using circles for dots over a lower-case i, or failing to indent paragraphs and underline headings. Drive them out of your writing.

Use a good quality writer-friendly pen with a reader-friendly dark blue or black ink. Take pride in your work!

Remember – this is nothing to do with whether you write 'joined-up' or 'print', but it is everything to do with whether you are legible and fluent. **Legible** means handwriting that is clear enough to read. **Fluent**, in the case of handwriting, means writing that flows freely.

Do not settle for poor handwriting.

The wake-up call

A BRIEF GUIDE TO COURSEWORK

'I can't <u>do</u> twenty page essays, so I've got <u>no</u> chance!'

Many students have the wrong idea about coursework. Coursework folders should not be filled with long, aimless pieces of work. Coursework pieces should generally be between three and five sides of A4 file paper. Your aim in coursework should be to show that your work is organized and well focused on the tasks set by your teacher at various stages of your course. Your coursework is not expected to be perfect, so do not expect your teacher to correct everything for you – she or he is not allowed to! Just make a steady effort and try to complete your folder to the best of your ability.

This book is mainly about helping students to prepare for the examination, and it makes sense to see your coursework as an ongoing opportunity to practise your exam skills. Therefore, you need to answer questions directly (not waffle for 20 pages!) and you need to proofread your work independently (not rely on your teacher for corrections!).

Frequently asked questions about coursework

'Is it true that I have to do 20 pieces of coursework?!'

No! Somebody's pulling your leg. You need four pieces for English and four for English Literature, and, in this case, four plus four adds up to SIX or SEVEN, because you can double-enter one or two of the Literature pieces in English.

'How much drafting should I do?'

In an exam you have no time to draft and rewrite, but in coursework you do. Fair enough, but keep it under control, for your own sanity! Your first reading or literature assignment may prove especially tricky, for example, and you are allowed general advice from your teacher about rearranging paragraphs and adding more detail, etc. For something like a story or letter, do your own proof-reading, and stick to one practice run.

'Can I word-process my coursework?'

Most of it, yes, but your teacher has to be sure that it is your work. There has to be some handwritten work in each folder and there also has to be a classroom supervised piece in each folder. Indeed, teachers need to know at all times in detail how your coursework is progressing. Word-processing is good for drafting and proof-reading, of course, and there's no problem if you genuinely develop those skills during the course.

'Can I use the Internet to help with my coursework?'

Good question. Be careful; be very, very careful! Be upfront and honest if you do get any ideas and material from the Internet. Don't be tempted to download a quick fix. Use your own words at all times. Candidates who use material that is not their own, without acknowledgement, risk severe penalties.

'What if I want to improve one of my pieces of reading/literature coursework later in the course?'

Not a good idea! One, after your teacher has marked a piece, it should not be rewritten. Two, revisiting longer texts (novels and plays) is very time-consuming and you would be wiser preparing for your exams. Three, the profit from a redone piece may at best be one or two marks. Have faith in your teacher (and this book) to prepare you for exam success!

Options and Specifications

The coursework bits!

In English, you will follow the England or the Wales coursework option. In English Literature, you will follow Specification A or Specification B.

Full details are shown on the next page. Your teacher, of course, will be familiar with the details and will guide you step-by-step through your particular coursework requirements.

All English and English Literature candidates have to write about different types of literature and also have to do different forms of writing. Here is a single piece of important advice on each type of work to send you on your way with coursework!

Poetry

Don't get too technical – use words you understand and ideas that are your own.

Prose

Don't retell the whole story – choose details that support the points you want to make.

Drama

Remember that it's a play you're writing about and it was designed to be performed – it's more than just the words on the page.

Imaginative/Descriptive writing (open)

Keep reasonably close to personal experience – try to engage the reader in the way you yourself would want to be interested.

Transactional/Discursive writing (closed)

Take it as real – make the language suitable for the intended audience and purpose.

Coursework outline

ENGLISH COURSEWORK
WALES OPTION

1. Reading: Welsh Relevance
2. Reading: Different Cultures
3. Writing: Narrative/Expressive
4. Writing: Informative/Persuasive

(One piece must be teacher supervised.)

(One Reading piece must be Poetry.)

(One Reading piece must be Drama.)

(One piece at least must be handwritten.)

ENGLISH COURSEWORK
ENGLAND OPTION

1. Reading: Shakespeare play
2. Reading: Different Cultures poetry
3. Writing: Narrative/Expressive
4. Writing: Informative/Persuasive

(One piece must be teacher supervised.)

(One piece at least must be handwritten.)

ENGLISH – SPEAKING AND LISTENING

1. Group discussion and interaction
2. Individual extended contribution
3. Drama focused activity

ENGLISH LITERATURE COURSEWORK
Specification A

1. Poetry
2. Poetry
3. Prose
4. Drama

Second prose text to be studied for exam.

Second drama text to be studied for exam.

(Pre-1914 and Post-1914 categories must be covered in each of poetry, prose and drama.)

(Two assignments must compare texts.)

ENGLISH LITERATURE COURSEWORK
Specification B

1. Poetry (pre-1914)
2. Prose (pre-1914)
3. Drama
4. Wider Reading

Second drama text to be studied for exam.

(Pre-1914 and Post-1914 categories must be covered in drama.)

(WJEC set anthology for Specification B covers post-1914 poetry and prose, and the comparative requirement.)

A five-point plan for coursework

Take this advice seriously

1 Follow your teacher's instructions closely and seek advice from him/her at every turn.

2 Do your coursework promptly, so that ideas are fresh in your head when you write. Do not under-perform early in the course.

3 Keep all of your notes, rough work and drafts as back-up. Even if you are word-processing, print out a draft and keep it, so that you can share the process as required with your teacher.

4 Take great care how you use the Internet for research. If any downloaded text plays a part in your assignment, print it out and keep it.

5 Remember that coursework is worth only 20% of the marks in English and 30% in English Literature. Treat it seriously, but do not allow it to dominate your efforts. See it as an opportunity to develop skills for the final exams.

Be as independent as you can in coursework, so that you can cope on your own in the exams.

Unit 0.3

Intelligent noise only!

A BRIEF GUIDE TO SPEAKING AND LISTENING

'I do speaking, but I don't do listening!'

Speaking and Listening work (Oral work or 'Oracy') should not be hit-and-miss. It counts for 20% of the marks in GCSE English and you have to earn them. There are rules and disciplines to follow on an everyday basis, and there are particular tasks to do and skills to show. It is your teacher who will, in effect, award you the mark for Speaking and Listening at the end of the course, so it makes sense to keep him or her 'sweet' along the way!

Speaking and listening is at the heart of your course in English and English Literature. You have to **take part** in a wide range of classroom tasks. You have to **communicate** clearly. You have to **show understanding** by listening and engaging.

If you don't listen, you don't learn. If you don't listen, your speaking, your writing and your understanding will suffer, because you will be out-of-step with the work, out-of-line with your teacher and out-of-order with your behaviour.

Assessment tasks

Discussion and Interaction – pairs and group work
Individual Extended Contribution – a talk or presentation
Drama-related Activity – playing a role

Every candidate has to be assessed in each of the three areas.
How do you feel about that?
Place them in order of preference for you personally.

Frequently asked questions about Speaking and Listening

'I'm really shy – do I have to stand in front of the whole class and give a talk?'

You do not have to stand up and it doesn't have to be the whole class! You do, though, have to speak at some length, though no more than five minutes is needed and you can sit down for it if you wish. It can be on a topic of personal interest or it can be a report from a group. It can be done alongside a friend, provided you do your fair share of the speaking. BUT if you do miss any part of Speaking and Listening, you will definitely lose credit.

'I've always messed around in English, but I've decided I want to join the police and I need a good grade. Will I be able to improve my mark in Speaking and Listening?'

Good day, constable. Welcome to the real world! Your first job is to persuade your teacher that you are serious and to get her or him on your side. You may or may not have enough time to make a difference. If you are close to the end of your course, your teacher might be persuaded to give you another chance to do an extended individual contribution – perhaps a talk to Year 10 could be arranged to tell them how to learn from your mistakes!

'Do Higher Tier candidates automatically get a better mark than Foundation Tier students for Speaking and Listening?'

No! Speaking and Listening marks are awarded on the same scale for both tiers and every individual should get the mark they have earned. There is almost certain to be an overlap of marks between any two classes and the two tiers. There is a system of double-checking (called moderation) to make sure that there is always another teacher to give a second opinion on the marks awarded.

Purposes of talk

When we talk we are generally trying to do one of nine things:

explain, describe, narrate
explore, analyse, imagine
discuss, argue, persuade.

You'll meet these terms throughout your GCSE course.

Ask yourself honestly:
- *Do I play a full and active part in all group discussions?*
- *Can I express my point of view constructively?*
- *Do I listen with concentration to the teacher and fellow students?*

If you can say, hand on heart, YES to:

3 out of 3	Your oral work is bound to help your GCSE grade(s).
2 out of 3	You are sensible enough to take stock and improve.
1 out of 3	You are in danger of under-achieving.
0 out of 3	You are probably a nuisance to your friends and peers.

Hiding your talents?

Do you personally use speaking and listening skills effectively in other school subjects? Which subjects? Which skills?

Do you use speaking and listening skills effectively in any out-of-school situations? Part-time job? Hobby? Leadership role?

You may be better than you think. Don't leave your skills outside the English classroom door!

Careers advice (not really)

Consider in detail the speaking and listening skills needed in the following occupations:

• taxi driver	• traffic warden	• surgeon
• opera singer	• hairdresser	• professional sportsperson.

Think of other jobs, including your own likely career choice. Can you think of any job where speaking and listening skills are not required?

Speaking and Listening – it's for grown-ups!

Unit 1.1

What are YOUR thoughts and feelings?

PERSONAL RESPONSE

'I can read, but I can't do comprehensions. I don't get many marks.'

When you are asked to give '**your** thoughts and feelings' about characters and situations, that is exactly what is meant – YOUR thoughts and feelings.

Begin at least some of your sentences with:

- I think....
- I feel...
- My thoughts are...
- My feeling is...

At GCSE, you have to learn to extend your answers to earn as many of the marks available as possible. Most of the questions on an extract of a story will be worth 10 marks. As a general rule, you must attempt to score the marks by building an answer. You must trawl through the passage, trying to pick up the points.

Very few candidates write 'wrong' answers in GCSE English, but many fail to keep their answers going for long enough.

The text

Read the following extract from the novel *Stone Cold* by Robert Swindells. It is about a youth called Link, who has run away from home and who is sleeping on the streets of London.

And don't forget the cold. If you've ever tried dropping off to sleep with cold feet, even in bed, you'll know it's impossible. You've got to warm up those feet, or lie awake. And in January, in a doorway, in wet trainers, it can be quite a struggle. And if you manage it, chances are you'll need to get up for a pee, and then it starts all over again.

And those are only some of the hassles. I haven't mentioned stomach cramps from hunger, headaches from the flu, toothache,

fleas and lice. I haven't talked about homesickness, depression or despair. I haven't gone into how it feels to want a girlfriend when your circumstances make it virtually impossible for you to get one – how it feels to know you are a social outcast in fact, a non-person to whom every ordinary everyday activity is closed.

So. You lie on your bruises, listening. Trying to warm your feet. You curl up on your side and your hip hurts, so you stretch out on your back so your feet stay cold and the concrete hurts your heels. You force yourself to lie still for a bit, thinking that'll help you drop off, but it doesn't. Your pack feels like a rock under your head and your nose is cold. You wonder what time it is. Can you stop listening now, or could someone still come? Distant chimes. You strain your ears, counting. One o'clock? It can't be only one o'clock, surely? I've been here hours. Did I miss a chime?

What's that? Sounds like breathing. Heavy breathing, as in maniac. Lie still. Quiet. Maybe he won't see you. Listen. Is he still there? Silence now. Creeping up, perhaps. No. Relax. Jeez, my feet are cold.

A thought out of nowhere – my old room at home. My little bed. What I wouldn't give for – no, mustn't. No sleep that way. Somebody could be asleep in that room right now. Warm and dry. Safe. Lucky sod.

Food. God, don't start on about food! (Remember that time in Whitby – fish and chip caff? Long, sizzling haddock, heap of chips like a mountain. So many, you had to leave some.) Wish I had them now.

Mum. Wonder what Mum's doing? Wonder if she wonders where I am? How would she feel if she knew? I miss you, Mum. Do you miss me? Does anybody?

Chimes again. Quarter past. Quarter past one? I don't believe it.

DSS. Are they considering my claim? (Not now they're not – they're sleeping. Snug as a bug in a rug.) Do they know what it feels like, kipping in a doorway? No.

And so it goes on, hour after hour. Now and then you doze a bit, but only a bit. You're so cold, so frightened and it hurts so much that you end up praying for morning even though you're dog-tired – even though tomorrow is certain to be every bit as grim as yesterday.

And the worst part is knowing you haven't deserved any of it.

The question

Now answer the following question:

- **What are your thoughts and feelings about Link's life on the streets?**

You must refer to the text to support the points you make.

> **Build your answer**
>
> - It is obviously important that you back up your thoughts and feelings with some kind of evidence to illustrate the points you make. This is what the second sentence of the question is advising you to do.
> - For practice, make a list of about ten different things to say. Then link your ideas and build them into sentences. In the exam, you write this kind of answer in paragraphs (not as a list).
> - Now write your answer. If you wish, you can read the answer below before you do so, but do not copy it out as your own! It is not intended as a perfect answer, and it does not contain all the points that could be made.

SAMPLE ANSWER

My thoughts of life on the streets I get when I read this extract is that it is cold because the writer starts telling us straight away that it is. And he tells us the date, which was January, which is in winter so it is obviously cold.

Another is that it would be very uncomfortable, he tells us he has pains in his hips and that the concrete hurts his heels. Also that he has to use his backpack as a pillow which he says feels like a rock. None of these would help you get to sleep but prevent it, so I feel that if living on the streets you would be tired and drowsy all the time.

Other hassles would be that you would be ill most of the time. Also the writer says that he's a social outcast and that gives the impression that people treat him as something lower than human. So I think that living on the streets would be very depressing.

I also get the impression that you would be anxious, always thinking about the time. I have often lain in bed not able to sleep and thinking of the time and eventually plucking up the courage to reach for my clock. Also it seems you would be scared and on your toes listening to noises as they pass. My overall feeling I get is that it would be a degrading position to be in, and a horrible experience.

COMMENT

This is a good 'personal response' answer that hovers between D and C grades. There is undoubtedly C grade potential in the answer, but overall it is rather inconsistent. To get a mark for a clear C you have to use textual details effectively as evidence to support thoughts and feelings.

The answer starts quite slowly, making the main and obvious point about the cold and adding 'January' and 'winter' to back this up. Lots of details are picked out in the second paragraph that help the point about 'uncomfortable' and then in the third paragraph points are made about being ill, being a social outcast and life on the streets being depressing. More is to come – the final paragraph covers the problems of sleeping and it ends with the student being confident enough to add his own opinion with strong phrases like 'degrading position' and 'horrible experience'.

Compare your answer with the one above. Did you make any points that were not in this answer?

THE BRAINWASH BOX

- Look closely at the words of the question.
- You can write 'I think...' and 'I feel...'.
- Build an answer with as many points as possible.
- Back up your points with details from the text.

Change the question

The following two-part English Literature question is similar to the one you have been asked to answer. Look out for 'impressions' instead of 'thoughts and feelings'.

- **What impressions of life on the streets do you have when you read this extract?**

  Choose parts of the extract that you find particularly effective in creating these impressions and write about them, explaining why you find them effective.

CHECKLIST

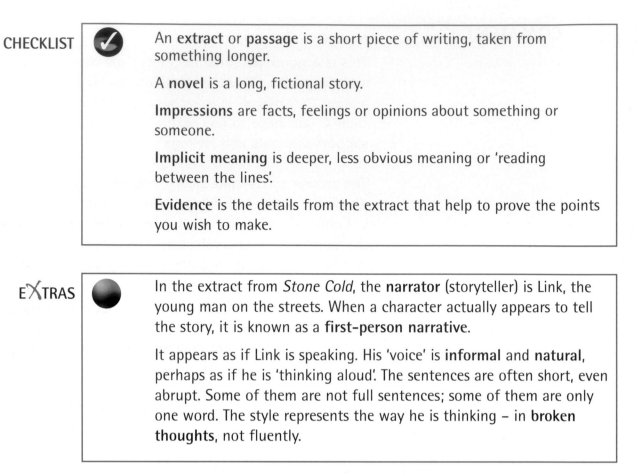

An **extract** or **passage** is a short piece of writing, taken from something longer.

A **novel** is a long, fictional story.

Impressions are facts, feelings or opinions about something or someone.

Implicit meaning is deeper, less obvious meaning or 'reading between the lines'.

Evidence is the details from the extract that help to prove the points you wish to make.

EXTRAS

In the extract from *Stone Cold*, the **narrator** (storyteller) is Link, the young man on the streets. When a character actually appears to tell the story, it is known as a **first-person narrative**.

It appears as if Link is speaking. His 'voice' is **informal** and **natural**, perhaps as if he is 'thinking aloud'. The sentences are often short, even abrupt. Some of them are not full sentences; some of them are only one word. The style represents the way he is thinking – in **broken thoughts**, not fluently.

Clock up as many relevant points as possible when you answer a question.

Unit 1.2

How do characters behave?

DEEPER MEANING

'I don't know where to start when I've got to answer a question like this. The answer either comes to you or it doesn't. You can either do it or you can't ... and I can't!'

You must have a method for working out deeper meaning. You must do the detective work on a character. You must systematically work through the lines of the story to find the key evidence...and then find something intelligent to say about some of it!

So, you need the hard work to get you in position – and then you need some confidence in yourself...

In the text that follows you are going to focus on a character who is a boss. It is worth considering what you might expect from a boss...or perhaps from some people who like to be bossy. You may have a picture in your head of a stereotype boss – in other words, someone who perhaps loves being the boss...and bossing people around. Then, you will need to look at the details about this particular boss and see in what ways he is the 'stereotype' and in what ways not.

The text

Read the following extract from the novel *Of Mice and Men* by John Steinbeck. George Milton and Lennie Small are travelling ranch labourers in 1930s America. They are being interviewed for work by the boss of a ranch. George is protective of Lennie because Lennie is not very bright.

The boss licked his pencil. 'What's your name?'

'George Milton.'

'And what's yours?'

George said, 'His name's Lennie Small.'

The names were entered in the book. 'Let's see, this is the twentieth, noon the twentieth.' He closed the book. 'Where you boys been working?'

'Up around Weed,' said George.

'You too?' To Lennie.

'Yeah, him too,' said George.

The boss pointed a playful finger at Lennie. 'He ain't much of a talker, is he?'

'No, he ain't, but he's sure a hell of a good worker. Strong as a bull.'

Lennie smiled to himself. 'Strong as a bull.' He repeated.

George scowled at him, and Lennie dropped his head in shame at having forgotten.

The boss said suddenly, 'Listen, Small!' Lennie raised his head. 'What can you do?'

In a panic, Lennie looked at George for help. 'He can do anything you tell him,' said George. 'He's a good skinner. He can rassel grain-bags, drive a cultivator. He can do anything. Just give him a try.'

The boss turned to George. 'Then why don't you let him answer? What you trying to put over?'

George broke in loudly, 'Oh! I ain't saying he's bright. He ain't. But I say he's a god-damn good worker. He can put up a four-hundred-pound bale.'

The boss deliberately put the little book in his pocket. He hooked his thumbs in his belt and squinted one eye nearly closed. 'Say – what you sellin'?'

'Huh?'

'I said what stake you got in this guy? You takin' his pay away from him?'

'No, 'course I ain't. Why ya think I'm sellin' him out?'

'Well, I never seen one guy take so much trouble for another guy. I just like to know what your interest is.'

George said, 'He's my . . . cousin. I told his old lady I'd take care of him. He got kicked in the head by a horse when he was a kid. He's awright. Just ain't bright. But he can do anything you tell him.'

The boss turned half away. 'Well, God knows he don't need any brains to buck barley bags. But don't you try to put nothing over, Milton. I got my eye on you. Why'd you quit in Weed?'

'Job was done,' said George promptly.

'What kinda job?'

'We . . . was diggin' a cesspool.'

'All right. But don't try to put nothing over, 'cause you can't get away with nothing. I seen wise guys before. Go on out with the grain teams after dinner. They're pickin' up barley at the threshing machine. Go out with Slim's team.'

'Slim?'

'Yeah. Big tall skinner. You'll see him at dinner.' He turned abruptly and went to the door, but before he went out he turned and looked for a long moment at the two men.

When the sound of his footsteps had died away, George turned on Lennie. 'So you wasn't gonna say a word. You was gonna leave your big flapper shut and leave me do the talkin'. Damn near lost us the job.'

Lennie stared hopelessly at his hands. 'I forgot, George.'

'Yeah, you forgot. You always forget, an' I got to talk you out of it.' He sat down heavily on the bunk. 'Now he's got his eye on us. Now we got to be careful and not make no slips. You keep your big flapper shut after this.'

The question

Now answer the following question:

- **How does the boss behave to George and Lennie in this extract?**

Consider:
- what the boss says and does
- how the boss says it and does it.

Using the bullet points

These are included to help you, so do not ignore them. In this case, you can see that 'behaves' in the question = 'says and does' in the bullet points.

Tracking the text

To answer this question effectively, you need to 'track the text'. This means you work through from the top to the bottom of the extract looking for any important references to the 'boss'.

Many exam candidates find it useful to underline bits of the text they wish to refer to. This is an excellent idea for keeping your focus on the task – BUT... you have to be quick.

You need to make important selections. For example:

> <u>The boss licked his pencil. 'What's your name?'</u>
> 'George Milton.'
> 'And what's yours?'
> George said, 'His name's Lennie Small.'
> <u>The names were entered in the book.</u> 'Let's see, this is the twentieth, noon the twentieth.' <u>He closed the book. 'Where you boys been working?'</u>
> 'Up around Weed,' said George.
> 'You too?' To Lennie.
> 'Yeah, him too,' said George.
> <u>The boss pointed a playful finger at Lennie. 'He ain't much of a talker, is he?'</u>

(A full version of the underlined text can be found in the *Teacher's Guide*.)

What might 'licked the pencil' suggest about the boss?

It might suggest that he is being business-like. Is he perhaps making a point from the start that he IS the boss, because he is behaving how he thinks a boss should?

In the following answer, the student decides not to mention that point, but makes other useful points in quite a long answer.

SAMPLE ANSWER

In the extract the boss acts in various ways towards George and Lennie. In the beginning the boss doesn't know what to think of Lennie as he says 'He ain't much of a talker is he?' Maybe he's thinking that he's hired a real duffer. This is backed up by the boss saying to Lennie 'What can you do?' and on saying this Lennie panics and George says that Lennie can do anything you tell him. The boss gets suspicious and says 'Then why don't you let him answer? What you trying to put over?' Showing that he thinks that Lennie is definitely not the worker he wanted if he can't even answer his own questions. George then tries to put the boss at ease and say 'Oh! I ain't saying he's bright. He ain't. But he is a god-damn good worker . . .' Then after that was said comes another different way in which the boss acts towards George and Lennie. The boss says 'Say – what you sellin'?' implying that George is trying to pull a sly one over the boss. Frustrated, the boss then tries to figure out what is going on with these two by asking why George is trying so hard to cover for Lennie. George then springs an answer and says that Lennie is Georges cousin and he had promised Lennies mum he'd look after him. He also adds that Lennie was kicked in the head by a horse as a kid. The boss buys this story and continues the questioning on trying to sus these guys out. The boss says ' . . . don't try to put nothing over, Milton. I got my eye on you.' Suggesting that still he believes these guys are up to something. He continues 'Why'd you quit in Weed?' again maybe curious why the men quit, perhaps the boss thinks that they did something up in Weed. George then answers, 'Job was done', covering up that they were chased out. The boss continues 'What kinda Job?' trying to dig deeper into what these men are all about.

COMMENT

This is a useful answer to study, because it does some things well and some things not so well. The length is good and there are some points that show understanding of the way the boss is behaving, but there are some parts where the focus on the boss is lost. The boss is never entirely forgotten in the answer, but there is just too much about George and Lennie. Remember that the question as it is worded is a 'boss' question, not a 'George and Lennie' question! You could consider crossing out any sentences that are entirely about the two men and not the boss.

THE BRAINWASH BOX
- Personal response is OK.
- Keep your answers going.
- Refer to the text.

Change the question!

- **How does George react when he is interviewed by the boss?**

Consider:
- what George says and does
- how George says it and does it.

CHECKLIST

✔ A **character** is a person in a novel, play or film.

A **stereotype** is a fixed image of someone. A stereotype is supposed to behave in a typical, predictable way.

Dialogue is conversation between two or more people within a story.

Tracking the text means working through the lines in an orderly way.

EXTRAS

The storyteller (or **narrator**) in *Of Mice and Men* stands outside the action and is the **observer** of what goes on. This is known as a **third-person narrative**. Note how this particular extract is dominated by **dialogue**, i.e. the characters are talking to each other.

It is not surprising that *Of Mice and Men* is also a successful play and film, because John Steinbeck's writing does draw out the characters as individuals. You are given lots of details about each of the characters.

Track the text methodically.

Look closely at the evidence...

HOW DOES THE WRITER...?

'How do I know? I'm not a writer, am I?'

Writers start with blank pieces of paper, just like we do when we begin to write. They fill the paper with words and sentences, cross some out, replace them, and change them around. They end with something they are reasonably happy with.

Do not be shy as the reader about commenting on what a writer has written: the words and phrases she or he has chosen; the organization of the sentences and paragraphs; the 'voice' that the writer has chosen to use for telling the story.

The text

Read the following extract from the novel *Paddy Clarke Ha Ha Ha* by Roddy Doyle. Paddy is a young boy growing up in Ireland in the 1960s.

We were flinging water at each other. We'd stopped laughing cos we'd been doing it for ages. The tide was going out so we'd be getting out in a minute. Edward Swanwick pushed his hands out and sent a wave towards me and there was a jellyfish in it. A huge see-through one with pink veins and a purple middle. I lifted my arms way up and started to move but it still rubbed my side. I screamed. I pushed through the water to the steps. I felt the jellyfish hit my back; I thought I did. I yelled again I couldn't help it. It was rocky and uneven down at the seafront, not like the beach. I got to the steps and grabbed the bar.

– It's a Portuguese man of war, said Edward Swanwick.

He was coming back to the steps a long way, around the jellyfish.

I got onto the second step. I looked for marks. Jellyfish stings didn't hurt until you got out of the water. There was a pink lash on the side of my belly; I could see it. I was out of the water.

– I'm going to get you, I told Edward Swanwick.

– It's a Portuguese man of war, said Edward Swanwick.

– Look at it.

I showed him my wound.

He was up on the platform now, looking over the railing at the jellyfish.

I took my togs off without bothering with the towel. There was no one else. The jellyfish was still floating there, like a runny umbrella. Edward Swanwick was hunting for stones. He went down some of the steps to reach for some but he wouldn't get back into the water. I couldn't get my T-shirt down over my back and chest because I was wet. It was stuck on my shoulders.

– Their stings are poisonous, said Edward Swanwick.

I had my T-shirt on now. I lifted it to make sure the mark was still there. I thought it was beginning to get sore. I wrung out my togs over the railing. Edward Swanwick was plopping stones near the jellyfish.

– Hit it.

He missed.

– You're a big spa, I told him.

I wrapped my togs in my towel. It was a big soft bath one. I shouldn't have had it.

I ran all the way, up Barrytown Road, all the way, past the cottages where there was a ghost and an old woman with a smell and no teeth, past the shops; I started to cry when I was three gates away from my house; around the back, in the kitchen door.

Ma was feeding the baby.

– What's wrong with you, Patrick?

She looked down for a cut on my leg. I got my T-shirt out to show her. I was really crying now. I wanted a hug and ointment and a bandage.

– A jelly – a Portuguese man of war got me, I told her.

She touched my side.

– There?

– Ouch! No, look; the mark across. It's highly poisonous.

– I can't see –. Oh, now I do.

I pulled my T-shirt down. I tucked it into my pants.

– What should we do? She asked me. – Will I go next door and phone for an ambulance?

– No; ointment –

– Okay, so. That'll mend it. Have I time for me to finish feeding Deirdre and Cathy before we put it on?

– Yeah.

– Great.

I pressed my hand hard into my side to keep the mark there.

The question

Now consider the following question:

- **How does the writer create a sense of childhood in this extract?**
  You must refer to the text to support the points you make.

This kind of question could be asked in English Literature as well as in English.

Quoting the text

When you are answering a question that asks 'How does the writer...?' or even if you are responding to the instruction 'Refer to words from the text', you need to use quotations.

Quotations within an answer look like this:

- Paddy described his jellyfish sting as a 'wound'. It implies that...
- We know the boys were messing around because in the very first sentence it says 'flinging water at each other'.
- After he has cried, Paddy says to his mum 'Ouch! No, look; the mark across. It's highly poisonous.' This suggests that Paddy...

When you are quoting, focus on the key words. If you are quoting one word, make sure that it is significant and that you have some comment to make about it. Do not quote for longer than one sentence.

Avoid limp statements like:

- The writer uses interesting and exciting words like '.........' (So, what's so interesting and exciting about those, then?!)
- The writer ends the story by saying '.........' (Yes, I know – I read it for myself!!)

Quoting is important, but you don't have to be obsessed by it. For variation and speed, you can refer in passing to something that happens in the text by **paraphrasing** (using some of your own words), **signposting** (directing the examiner efficiently in your words to a part of the text) or **summarizing** (making a reference to a larger part of a text).

In the following answer, the student succeeds in creating the sense of childhood by linking the passage to what children do generally.

SAMPLE ANSWER

The story is slightly rushed as a child would do. Also the language the writer has used 'Ma was feeding the baby' or 'You're a big spa'.

From the first sentence you get a feel of childhood 'we were flinging water at each other.'

This is what children do at the beach, instantly you get the feeling of a warm and happy day at the beach.

Children are more dramatic than adults. In the story when Patrick gets stung by the jellyfish, instantly Edward thought of the most dangerous jellyfish – a Portuguese man of war. 'It's a Portuguese man of war' and 'Their stings are poisonous.' Also instead of Edward worrying about Patricks sting he decided to throw stones at the jellyfish. 'Edward Swanwick was plopping stones near the jellyfish'.

When children have cuts or injure themselves they want as much sympathy as possible. When Patricks mum told him she would get some ointment for his sting, Patrick started pressing his cut to make it look worse. 'I pressed my hand hard into my side to keep the mark there.'

COMMENT

This is an answer that shows a lot of promise, because the student attempts quite a wide range of points. Unfortunately, she tends to let the points go without completing them. For example, the very first comment is a vague one – does she wish to comment on the story being told through the eyes of the child? Elsewhere, too, she could mention that the boys were 'messing around, like children do' and make other such comments.

There is certainly more that could be said, for example by inserting comments into each paragraph.

Try it – add one sentence to each paragraph to explain what is already there. The result will be a clear grade C answer.

THE BRAINWASH BOX

- Personal response is OK.
- Keep your answers going.
- Refer to the text.
- Underline key words and phrases on your exam paper.
- Use short quotations.
- Make comments about your quotations.

Change the question!

- **What are your thoughts and feelings towards Paddy now you have read the whole passage? How does the writer make you feel this?**

Consider:
- what happens in the passage
- the relationships between the characters
- the writer's use of language.

CHECKLIST

A **quotation** (or **quote**) is a group of words taken from a text and used elsewhere. The quotation can normally be identified when **quotation marks** '......' are placed before and after the group of words.

Structure is the way a writer builds and organizes a piece of writing.

Style means the way the writer has chosen to write something.

Technique is the name often given to the skills and tricks that the writer uses in a piece of writing.

The **viewpoint** (or **perspective**) is a position from which a story is being told.

EXTRAS

The **viewpoint** (or **perspective**) of *Paddy Clarke Ha Ha Ha* is that of the 10 year-old Paddy. The actual writer is Roddy Doyle who used his own first-hand experience of Dublin in the 1960s to make the story real. The reader imagines getting into the head of the young boy, who, of course, does not always understand what is happening to him. The reader, meanwhile, can often work out exactly what is going on.

Use short, precise quotations and comment on them.

Unit 1.4

Imagine you are...

EMPATHY

'I don't have any imagination!'

Empathy tasks do require you to 'Imagine you are...' but they are tasks that test your reading and understanding – the material for your answer always lies within the lines of the text you are reading.

There are some obvious similarities with other reading questions:
- tracking the text
- selecting key details
- reading between the lines for deeper meaning
- showing some understanding of the whole text.

But there are also some obvious differences from other types of question:
- When you use 'I', you mean the character, not you, the candidate.
- You don't need to quote – instead you tend to 'echo' the text.
- Because you are 'inside a character's head', you are less likely to report the action in 'straight lines'.

The text

Read the extracts from the short story 'The New Boy' by Geddes Thomson. The story deals with the reactions of Tam, who immediately sees the new boy, Colin, as a rival.

There are four extracts from the story:
1. Tam's arrival at school and seeing the new boy for the first time
2. an English lesson
3. a PE/Games lesson
4. after school on that first day.

(The full story forms part of the English Literature Anthology used by GCSE English Literature Specification B candidates.)

Tam was in a good mood that morning. His mum had had a big win at the bingo the night before. She had brought home some special fish suppers, two bottles of Irn Bru and a big red box of chocolates. A nice surprise on a Tuesday night, with the rain running down the windows, no money for the gas fire and the telly rotten as usual.

She had given Tam five one pound notes which now nestled in his jerkin pocket. It was a great feeling, pound notes in your pocket. He would pass the day thinking about what he would do with all that money. Better than listening to moany old teachers.

He was explaining all this to his mate, Alec, as they dragged their feet through the school gate, when he first saw the new boy.

Tam nudged Alec. 'Whose zat?'

'Doan know. Never seen im before.'

The new boy was surrounded by a crowd of first years. He was a big broad-shouldered lad with a sun-tanned face and dark curly hair. He was dressed in a fancy pullover and brown corduroys and he was wearing a tie. The first years seemed to be enjoying his company, because they were laughing and skipping about him like a pack of playful dogs.

***

Today Mr Campbell was on about TV adverts, asking the class for their favourites. Tam, aware of the new boy somewhere behind him, put up his hand.

'Ah like the one about biscuits, Sir.'

Mr Campbell smiled encouragingly.

'Tell us about it, Tam.'

'Well it's these Mexican bandits an they rob a bank an the federales come an it's fur this biscuit.'

'I know the one you mean. Why do you like it?'

Tam decided to show off, show the new boy how gallus he was.

'Well, ah like the burds, Sir. Lovely burds in that ad.'

Alec spluttered with laughter, but Mr Campbell was not so easily put off. '*Why* do they have – young ladies – in the advert?'

There was a pause. 'Yes, Colin?'

Tam heard the voice of the new boy behind him. 'It's tae mak ye think the product is… glamorous. Tae…tae connect it wae nice ideas so that ye'll gae oot an buy it.'

Everybody turned round to look. They realized that he had put into words what had been vaguely going through their own minds.

Mr Campbell was delighted. 'That's a very good answer, Colin. A *very* good answer.'

But Colin wasn't finished yet. 'Tak this lassie aside me, Sir. Now if she was tae recommend biscuits oan the TV, I wid definitely buy them because she looks saw nice.'

Tam narrowed his eyes and glared. Kathy Milligan's dark head was lowered, but he could see her blush and smile. He had quite fancied Kathy Milligan for a long time and here was this character giving her the patter already.

*   *   *

Out in the playground they were divided into teams. Tam was pleased to see that he was in the opposite team from the new boy. Now he would show him who was the boss.

The game started. The orange football began to skid around the playground chased by the players.

After a few minutes the new boy, who turned out be a good player, dribbled towards Tam. As he went past Tam tripped him, making it look like an accidental late tackle. The new boy fell his full length on the concrete playground. His nose was in a puddle and his knee was bleeding. The white shorts were splattered with mud.

Big Sim came pounding up, blowing his whistle and waving his arms like a big-time referee as the boys crowded round the figure on the ground.

'Get back you lot. Are you OK lad? Any damage?'

The new boy smiled. 'Ah'm fine, Sir. Ah've just skint ma knee. That's aw. Accidents happen, ye ken.'

But Tam sensed that the rest of them didn't think it was an accident. He heard Alec's whisper over his left shoulder. 'See you. You're mental!'

For the rest of the game he hardly got a kick at the ball, but the new boy's name began to ring out over the playground.

'Well done, Colin.'

'Nice pass, Colin.'

'Great goal, Colin.'

Afterwards, in the dressing-room, Tam pulled on his clothes without a word to anybody. He felt that somehow he had suffered a great defeat and he wasn't quite sure how it had happened. OK, he had tripped the guy. So what? That was nothing.

*   *   *

Tam rose to his feet in the dark shelter. Slowly he walked out into the sunlight. The new boy saw him. He was waving something in his hand.

'Can ah see ye a meenit?' he shouted in that funny accent which grated on Tam's nerves.

'Ah suppose you can,' Tam shouted back, 'unless you're blind.'

The new boy was now standing in front of him. Alec was right. He *was* big. Tam had to look up into the broad brown face.

'The bigger they are the harder they faw.' That was what he had told Alec. It had been a favourite saying of his father's. 'The bigger they are the harder they faw.'

Tam clenched his fists inside his jerkin pockets.

'Something wrang?' the new boy asked.

'Aye,' Tam said. '*You're* wrang. You've been wrang since the minute ah saw ye. Who are you? Where do you come fae?'

The new boy opened his mouth to answer and, at that moment, Tam jumped him in a flurry of swirling arms and thudding fists. He heard the new boy gasp in pain, but he also felt knuckles crash into his own face. Desperately, he grabbed his enemy round the waist and the two of them swayed and tottered round the playground like two drunk men until they crashed to the ground.

Tam had him locked round the waist in a vice-like grip, but the new boy had an equally strong hold on Tam's neck.

After a minute like this he heard Colin MacDonald say, 'You let me go and ah'll let *you* go.'

Tam strengthened his grip while he thought about this. It might be a trick. On the other hand, Tam could feel his strength slowly draining away. He decided he had better take the offer while there was still time.

'One – two – three!' And Tam let go and at the same moment felt the arms drop away from his own neck.

They lay side by side on the hard playground. Exhausted.

'Yer a bonny fighter,' he heard the new boy say.

'Yer no sae bad, yersel,' Tam had to admit.

'Oh an ah've goat something fur ye,' Colin MacDonald sat up and opened his big brown fist to reveal a heap of green paper. 'Ah fund them in the dressing-room. They're yours, aren't they? Ah wis comin tae gie them tae yi.'

The pound notes. No longer new and crinkly, but crushed and dirty.

They grinned at each other.

The question

Now consider the following task:

- **Imagine you are Tam**. Later the same day you meet up with your friend Alec. You tell him what has happened and what you think of the new boy. Write down what you say.

Remember that this is a test of understanding and your answer must be closely linked to the text.

Overview – the whole story

Usually, in an empathy task you are **looking back**. The most effective way to do this is to establish the 'big idea' immediately. Tam ends the story on better terms with Colin and it is fair to say that he has changed his attitude to Colin.

Here are two possible opening sentences for your response to this empathy task. The first of them is satisfactory, but the second is better. Can you work out why?

> *I went to school happy this morning with the five pounds my mum gave me, but when I saw the new boy...*

> *I've changed my mind about Colin 'cos he's quite a good lad really...*

Highlighting – selecting the key details

This text here is rather longer than a typical examination extract, so there is plenty of detail to choose from. In fact, you're spoilt for choice!

When writing an answer, empathy question or not, you are not expected to get the 'full house' of details. In this particular task, however, you should really comment on:
- the fight and the money
- the football match (tripping him up)
- the English lesson (feeling jealous, thinking him a bighead)
- seeing him for the first time (feeling threatened?).

The 'voice' of the character

It is very difficult here to adopt the character's voice, as he speaks in a Scots accent and dialect, but any attempt to pick up a conversational style would be in your favour. You could, however, write a thoroughly convincing answer without adopting dialect or colloquial language.

Do not:

- write a response that begins 'If I were Tam, I would be...'. This is not a direct route. It is not possible, using 'If I were...', to sound like the character himself.
- write a dialogue or playscript when only the contribution of one character is required.

SAMPLE ANSWER

ALEC: What do you think of Colin now?
TAM: Well I've changed my mind.
ALEC: Why?
TAM: We had a fight.
ALEC: You had a fight?
TAM: Yes, we had a fight!

COMMENT

Zzzzzzzzzz! Too slow! Even if it were quicker, Alec's contribution would deflect from the purpose of your response. His job is to listen!

Do:

- write like this...

SAMPLE ANSWER

'I guess I have to admit I'd got it in for him from the moment I saw him this morning. It seemed as if he was showing off to the littl'uns and I just felt he'd got my space. I wasn't really thinking it through... Then in English he got my glory. There was me thinking I was clever...
But...

COMMENT

This is clearly heading for a C grade, provided it is sustained for nearly a side of A4 paper. It is using detail from different parts of the text and beginning to sound like Tam, at least in the way he shows he has understood his own fear and jealousy of the new boy.

THE BRAINWASH BOX

- Speak directly as the character.
- Think like the character.
- Get the character's feelings.
- Remember you are looking back from the end of the story.

Change the question!

- **Imagine you are Colin**. You tell your mother about your first day at your new school. Write down what you say.

Remember that this is a test of understanding and your answer must be closely linked to the text.

CHECKLIST ✔

'The New Boy' contains a lot of dialogue (speech) and the story is made more real by the way the writer tries to represent the Scots accent and dialect. Tam thinks that Colin speaks strangely, but Tam also speaks with a regional variation of English, i.e. Scots. Note that Mr Campbell speaks Standard English.

Standard English is English that is spoken or written to society's broadly agreed rules of grammar. You can use Standard English without being 'posh'.

An **accent** is a distinctive way of pronouncing the words you speak in English. You can, though, speak Standard English with an accent. It's only the sounds that are different.

A **dialect** is a local or a regional variation of Standard English when the words and/or the rules of grammar are changed.

In 'The New Boy', the strange spellings are a mixture of accent and dialect.

E X TRAS

> The **short story** in literature is something much shorter than a novel and therefore it cannot cover as much ground as a novel. Short stories, however, are sometimes up to 50 pages long and sometimes long enough to be a mini-novel or **novella**.
>
> Short stories tend to focus on **a single incident, moment in time, or experience**, but look out for different approaches, even in stories of five or so pages.
>
> As with a novel, you will be expected to be interested in **plot and structure, narrative viewpoint, characters** and **language and style**.
>
> A short story can have **great impact and effect** simply because it has such a **sharp focus** on its subject.

EMPATHY tasks test your READING skills.

Pictures in words

DESCRIPTIVE WRITING

'I can't do descriptive writing. You have to know about adjectives and adverbs and stuff ... and the titles are always boring. I just don't know how to do it ...'

Descriptive writing in the exam requires you to write about a place or a person. Often when you are asked to write about a particular place, you will naturally include people in your description of the place. The key thing to remember is to focus on the scene (or the character portrait). You should not tell a story.

So, you need to be focused and you also need to be a little bit individual. Or, to put it another way, you need to avoid being general. For example, in a crowded school dining room, it is likely that some people might be shouting and some might be eating quietly, so do not write 'Everybody was shouting'.

Be realistic in your description – how often do you hear patients screaming out in pain and fear when they visit the dentist? Answer: never! So don't write 'The patient was screaming...'!

Adjectives and adverbs? They are the so-called descriptive words that describe nouns and verbs:

> The **young** boy bolted his **greasy** food **greedily** and left **quickly**.

If you overdo this kind of description, it becomes obvious that you are 'writing by numbers' or working to a tired formula, rather than using a picture in your head. Adjectives and adverbs are useful when used selectively, not frequently.

The task

Consider the following descriptive writing task:

- **Describe a scene at a train or bus station.**

Get focused

You should write about a page in your answer book. Remember that this is a test of your ability to write descriptively, so focus on the place or person you have been asked to write about. Do not write a story.

Imagine a scene at a train or bus station and create a picture in words.

You can describe people, use names, use speech, use a range of senses, talk about the weather, and create movement and action.

You should not overuse adjectives and adverbs. You should also try not to generalize or lose hold of reality.

You can put yourself into the scene or you can be on the outside of it.

There is a sample answer below, which you can either read now or after you have attempted the task yourself.

In this answer the writer focuses very successfully on the train station. Whatever the situation, you have to think about which approach will work most effectively...for **you**.

SAMPLE ANSWER

I arrive just as my train is leaving and the next train I can catch isn't for another hour. I'm stuck in Cardiff train station in the dark and freezing cold. No one else about for me to talk to. I wander around, reading the graffiti written on the benches, 'Meg Loves Chris' and 'Peter 4 Louise'. I'm thinking the next time Meg comes here she's probably not going to be in love with Chris. As I sit down next to a 'Stewie is gay' graffiti tag, I hear some chants coming from the corridor below the platform. All of a sudden there is an atmosphere being generated by 50 or so football fans, singing and shouting songs about opposition players.

The station announcer announces that the train will be delayed by ten, fifteen minutes.

It's started to rain and it's heavy at that. The shops are closing soon and the platform is already busy. I glance over and see a homeless man with a bottle of whisky, which probably keeps him warm. His old grey duffle coat is looking worse for wear, holes in the sleeve and pockets. Judging by the vomit caked in his long scruffy beard he has not been well. Then one of the football fans, who is a bit drunk himself, starts aiming insults at the homeless man. He may be drunk, but the homeless man gives as good as he gets, leaving the rowdy fan quite stunned. When he gets back to his friends he gets a right old ribbing for being out-insulted by the homeless man.

COMMENT

This piece of descriptive writing is definitely constructed out of the student's own experience and is all the better for it. Cardiff is mentioned, which helps the reader's sense of place, but the touches of descriptive detail do most to create the feeling of a bleak, unattractive scene. The student decides to write this piece using 'I', the first person 'voice', and does so effectively, avoiding the temptation of writing a story about himself. He uses the present tense consistently throughout the piece – this creates a sense of immediacy and drama (as if the action is happening NOW).

Even though this is definitely not a story, there is a sense of something happening – some action and some interesting observations. There is scope for better use of vocabulary in places. Can you spot where? Can you spot any other opportunities?

The sentences, punctuation and spelling are generally accurate, and the overall piece is worth a C grade.

Make a list of the good points and a list of the weaknesses in the sample piece of writing above.

THE BRAINWASH BOX

- Focus on the scene.
- Don't tell a story.
- Don't generalize.
- Don't overdose on adjectives and adverbs.

Change the question!

- **Describe the scene in an examination hall.**

You should write about a page in your answer book. Remember that this is a test of your ability to write descriptively.

CHECKLIST ✔

A **noun** is a naming word. It can be a person, a place or a thing.
A **verb** is a word (or a group of words) that indicates an action or a state of being.
An **adjective** is a word that describes or adds to the meaning of a noun.
An **adverb** is a word that modifies or adds to the meaning of a verb or an adjective or another adverb.

First-person refers to the narrator or storyteller when 'I' or 'we' is used.
Second-person refers to 'you', which is occasionally used as the narrator in short descriptive writing.
Third-person refers to 'he', 'she', 'it', or 'they' as the narrator or storyteller.

The **verb tense** tells the time of the action of a sentence – in simplest terms: past, present or future.

EXTRAS ●

Any description is **subjective** – in other words, it is the writer's own view of a scene. It is possible to **highlight** certain features at the expense of others, and also to **understate** ('play down') some things while **exaggerating** others.

Each choice of a word can be crucial – a single student could be described as 'confident', 'cheeky', 'unruly', or 'outspoken', each description offering a **connotation** or suggested meaning. Each one of those words has a slightly different shade of meaning.

Use a picture in your head – bring a scene to life.

Unit 2.2 — Telling a tale

IMAGINATIVE WRITING

'Why do we have to write stories in the exam? I don't have any imagination and, anyway, isn't it a bit childish? None of us are going to write stories in the real world ...'

Writing a story (or a narrative) is not childish at all – in fact, it's the opposite. It's a test of maturity, and if you write something that is silly and childish, you will not a get a high mark. You have to try and write in as adult a way as possible. It may be artificial to ask you to write a story in 30–40 minutes, but your writing skills are being examined as well – under pressure.

Don't knock storytelling – we all do it every day of our lives. From ancient history to up-to-the-minute gossip, storytelling keeps the world going round.

Before you start

There is no set way in which everybody can write a good imaginative piece, but there is some good safety-first advice.

- Use as much time as you need to plan (in your head, if you wish) what you want to write.

- Starting immediately is unnecessary and, even if you do get a good idea straightaway, pause for a minute to reassure yourself that it will work well for you.

- Make sure that you know the direction in which your writing is going and even how it is going to end.

- Time left at the end of the 40 minutes (e.g. 15 to 20 minutes) can never be recovered, but time spent in thought at the beginning is never wasted.

- In fact, the most important part of your story is probably the opening. You are in control at the start and you might stay in control until the end. Even if you don't, you will have created a good impression at first.

Knowing your strengths

Are you someone who finds it easy to dream up a story out of thin air? Or do you prefer to stay close to your own experience? Using your imagination can mean rediscovering a personal memory and retelling it. You do not need to create an adventure, a mystery, a thriller or a fantasy – a piece of writing based on an everyday event is fine.

Generally, realistic stories are more successful, although there are absolutely no rules and restrictions for using the prompts. What will you decide to do with one of the following choices?

The task

Consider the following imaginative writing task:

- **Choose ONE of the following and write between one and two sides of A4 paper in response.** Do this task in about 40 minutes.

    a) Write about an incident that taught you a valuable lesson.

    b) Loneliness. Write about an incident, real or imaginary, based on the feeling of loneliness.

    c) The Undiscovered Country.

    d) Write a story that ends with the words: 'And I crossed my fingers, praying my little white lie would not be detected.'

    e) The Slide.

    f) Write a story that begins with the words: 'It was not the brightest thing that I had ever done. In fact, this was another fine mess I was in...'

If you want some tips before you write an answer, read on. There are two sample openings to look at.

SAMPLE OPENING

It was not the brightest thing that I had ever done. In fact, this was another fine mess I was in.

I was in the middle of nowhere with nothing. My parents said this would happen if I went looking for him, but I thought differently. All that I wanted to do is look for Dan and find him, we had tried everything, leaving food overnight, but every morning we would wake up and find the food had gone, but there was no sign of Dan. It was one thing when I left the gate open so Dan could get out, but now I was lost as well.

I decided I would try and find my way back so I turned around and followed the flattened grass which I had already walked over. While I was walking back I kept calling for Dan but there was still no sign. Everything was fine, I was walking back and I could clearly see where I had been walking in the grass, but as I got further down the mountain I could see many other paths just like mine, this is where I must have gone wrong...

COMMENT

This student (Tom) chooses the prompt of a given opening sentence or two and sets off on a believable, realistic story about losing a pet. The first paragraph is really successful in interesting the reader, and the second paragraph takes the story on quickly so there is plenty to keep us guessing. What do you think of it? Should Tom have stuck with the tale of the lost pet, rather than getting lost himself? Where did that mountain come from? Where could he go with this story? Is he trying to do too much?

SAMPLE OPENING

The Undiscovered Country

Shel opened her eyes and saw that she was still sitting in the same seat on the aeroplane. It was a good job that she had put her seatbelt on when she realized that the pilot had lost control.

Inside the small aircraft everything had been thrown onto the floor and out of place. All the oxygen masks were dangling from the open compartments on the ceiling. Lights were smashed and vegetation was growing in from the open windows and doors. She sat there listening to the interesting noises beyond the creaking wreckage, there were birds squawking, insects buzzing and frogs croaking...

COMMENT

This student (Emilie) takes on the challenge of a title that seems to encourage a fictional story. She very carefully sets the scene and provokes the reader's interest by actually holding back information about the situation being described. We guess this is about a crashed plane, but we do not become overloaded with all the usual details of mangled wreckage. In fact, we see it all slowly through the eyes of the narrator (storyteller) looking around, undoubtedly dazed and confused. The details given are very effective and the whole scene is convincing. The questions are: How can Emilie keep this going? Will she try to go too far in a couple of pages of writing?

Exam tips

- Use descriptive detail in your story in the way that Emilie does in the story opening above.

- Focus on a main idea as Tom does in his opening paragraph, but try to keep that focus for longer than he does.

Now read a full sample response and comment thoughtfully on it. It has C grade potential, but falls into grade D.

SAMPLE ANSWER

Write about an incident that taught you a valuable lesson.

It was a crisp morning, the clouds were low and the air was cold. I stood wrapped up ready for another unenjoyable day. Yesterday I was told my best friend had been talking about me to the more popular girls in the school. It clung to my mind all night and it was still there playing with me as I wondered why on earth would she have done this to me.

My bus arrived, I got on. 'Rachel' my so called best friend shouted from the back of the bus 'I have saved a seat for you babe.'

Why was she acting all nice to me as if she had done nothing wrong? Ignoring her I sat at the front on my own. I felt a tap on my shoulder.

'What is wrong?' Rachel questioned.

'What do you mean what is wrong? It's who is in the wrong that you should be worried about!' I confronted Rachel. She looked at me red faced and confused. I explained to her what I had been told and all she could do was laugh in my face.

'I told those girls how much of a special friend you are to me and that I wouldn't leave you to hang around with those low lives!' Rachel exclaimed.

'If you want to believe them over me then go do so but you're on your own.'

I looked to the ground in disappointment. I still wondered who to believe. But then it became clear. I trusted Rachel with everything, there was nothing I didn't tell her. I knew she wouldn't leave me to wander the school on my own being made a laughing stock. But it was things which made me think twice about who I could trust after family problems at home.

I met up with Rachel later that afternoon, I told her how sorry I was and talked to her about my problems and how I find it hard to trust people. She sat and understood everything I had to say better than before.

I learned a very valuable lesson at this moment of time, And that is not to listen to hear say from others but to trust and believe your closest friends and not to judge them.

COMMENT

What is good and what is not so good about the story above?

Look at it in detail. How could it be improved? How could it be made more interesting for the reader?

Think about:
*   content and organization
*   sentence structure, punctuation and spelling.*

(*Sentence structure, punctuation and spelling are dealt with fully in Units 2.3 and 4.3.)

THE BRAINWASH BOX

*   Think hard at the start.
*   Don't write too much.
*   Control the ending.

Change the question!

- **Choose ONE of the following and write between one and two sides of A4 paper in response**. Do this task in about 40 minutes.

   a) Write a story in which someone stands up for his or her beliefs.

   b) Write a story about an incident that taught you the value of money.

   c) Running Scared.

   d) Write a story which ends with the following: '...It was all I could do to keep a straight face.'

   e) Continue the following: 'He never thought he would make the front page of the newspapers...'

CHECKLIST ✓ | **Imaginative** writing can be **fictional** or **realistic**.

Imaginative: *being creative, thinking of ideas*

Fictional (or fictitious): *a 'made-up' story*

Realistic: *true to life*

A title, an opening or an idea is a **writing prompt** to get you going.

EXTRAS ● | A **genre** is a particular type of writing, e.g. **poetry**, **drama**, **prose**.

Genre fiction is the name given to types of novel that can be easily categorized, e.g. romance, horror, science-fiction, mystery, fantasy. On the whole, these kinds of writing do not work well in an exam because they so often depend on complicated plots.

In contrast, **autobiographical** and **travel writing** do work well for exam candidates. With autobiography, there is the opportunity to use **personal history and public events**, as well to experiment with **the process of remembering**. Mystery and suspense can come from ordinary, everyday events in the best of writing.

Travel writing is less common, but students write well about places they have experienced and people they have met. Make sure, however, that you do not describe at length the outward journey to a holiday destination – and then run out of time! Put yourself in the place straightaway and create a **sense of place**.

Think your writing through to the end before you start.

Unit 2.3

The weakest link?

TECHNICAL ACCURACY

Sentences and punctuation

' Yeah, I use full stops and commas. Some days I use full stops and some days I use commas ...'

Punctuation is neither guesswork, nor decoration – it is a vital part of sentence control. It is tied in closely with the construction of the sentences themselves. If your punctuation is dodgy, it is likely that your sentence construction will be too.

If you have bad habits in your writing, it is NOT too late to change. Here is a brief guide to help you to improve your understanding of sentences and punctuation.

Sentence...or not?

A sentence is a sequence of words that makes sense. You need a full stop at the end of a sentence. You also need a properly formed verb to complete a sentence. A sequence of words that has good sense and a full stop, but which does not have a full verb, is called a minor sentence. Look at this list:

Children.	MINOR SENTENCE
Children in the street.	MINOR SENTENCE
Children playing in the street.	MINOR SENTENCE
Children **are** playing in the street.	**SENTENCE**

Minor sentences should be used with care. You need to show in your writing that you can use a range of properly constructed sentences. Do not let minor sentences dominate your descriptive writing.

Task 1

Copy each item and write down alongside whether it is a sentence or a minor sentence.

1. A crowded waiting room.
2. Children climbing over the chairs.
3. The clock strikes nine.
4. The door opens.
5. No seats available.

Simple sentences

A simple sentence is a sentence with only one verb. You would normally expect a short sentence, but a simple sentence can sometimes be quite long. For example:

*Liza **opened** the door.*

*Her tired mother with two huge bags of shopping **stood** there.*

Task 2

Each of the following items contains two or three simple sentences that must be separated by full stops. Write them out correctly.

1. I waited calmly, as usual my brother was late, fortunately it was a nice, sunny day.
2. The day drags on in school, everyone waits for the bell to ring there is no laughter here.
3. Finally the bell rings, with a sigh of relief, we go home.

CHECKLIST

A **conjunction** joins words, phrases or sentences together.

A **verb** shows the *action* or the *being* of a sentence. It can follow the word 'to' as in 'to be', 'to walk', but verbs have different forms, like 'was', 'has been', 'walks' and 'is walking'.

Compound sentences

A compound sentence is one in which two (or more) simple sentences are joined by one of the following conjunctions: **and**, **but**, **or**. For example:

*The sky was blue **and** the sun shone.*

*The sun shone **but** it was cold.*

*We could have a game of football **or** we could go fishing.*

Task 3

Make the following pairs of simple sentences into compound sentences.

1. The weatherman forecast sunny periods. It rained.
2. I could do my homework. I could go out with my friends.
3. We have a new teacher. He teaches English.
4. I was looking forward to seeing Eric. He was out.
5. Rachel passed all of her exams. She went out to celebrate.

Complex sentences

A complex sentence does not have to be a difficult or complicated sentence. It is, however, a sentence that is in some way constructed upon a simple or compound sentence.

One of the more straightforward ways of constructing a complex sentence is to use one of the following conjunctions:

when   because   if   although   as   while   after
before   since   unless   where   until   that

For example:

When *the dentist came into the waiting room, everyone held their breath for a second.*

Terry was forced to apologize **because** *his behaviour was poor.*

(Provided the sense of the sentence is ok, the conjunction can occur at the start of the sentence or in the middle.)

Because *his behaviour was poor, Terry was forced to apologize.*

Everyone held their breath for a second **when** *the dentist came into the waiting room.*

Task 4

Fill each gap with one of the conjunctions listed above.

1. Leah has been afraid of the dark _____ she watched that horror film.
2. _____ Danny learned to swim, he would not be allowed in the deep end.

3. Dawn made the coffee _____ I answered the phone.

4. Tony nudged his sister _____ their mother turned her back.

5. _____ Sian was tired, she didn't give up and she eventually won the competition.

6. _____ global warming is significant, there will be more incidents of extreme weather conditions in Britain.

7. You cannot say _____ I didn't warn you.

8. You will electrocute yourself _____ you connect those wires correctly.

9. Ian had to complete his homework _____ he could go out.

10. _____ he was injured, Freddie had to return home.

EXTRAS

● SENTENCES

Taking care with meaning

When you try hard to construct interesting sentences, watch out for problems with **word order** and **connections**!

For example:

Emma liked eating beef burgers more than her friends.

While photographing the elephants, the monkeys were leaping around in the cage behind us.

The dentist told the patient that he would not feel a thing.

Full stops and capital letters

A full stop marks the end of a sentence. A capital letter must be used at the start of each sentence.

It is a common failing for students to use a comma to separate sentences. This is called comma splicing and it is wrong!

Task 5

Sort out the punctuation in each of the items below. Be prepared to insert full stops and to replace commas. Shorten sentences and replace words if you wish.

1. The stairs inside the stadium were crowded with people rushing to get to their seats, it was the match that everyone had been talking about.

2. When I got to my block I walked up the stairs, and saw a sea of red shirts all around me, I could feel the excitement building up to the kick-off.

3. The whole crowd then erupted he had scored and Wales were winning the cheers rang louder than I have ever heard, the whole place was jumping with excitement.

4. All that Wales had to do now was play it safe the whistle blew for half-time, we had scored at just the right time.

5. The guitars were still feeding back and making a shocking noise, I wanted to get closer to the stage. Suddenly there was a big crash from one of the cymbals, and they started playing another song most people started jumping up and down at the same time, but there were a few people who couldn't jump they were just wedged in the crowd to fill a gap.

E**X**TRAS

FULL STOPS

Full stops are also used after **abbreviations** and **initials**.

For example: *Man. U. is used as an abbreviation for Manchester United.*

Note: The alternative abbreviation **Utd** for United has no full stop, because it ends with the same letter as the full spelling.

E**X**TRAS

CAPITAL LETTERS

Capital letters are also used for **proper names**, **titles**, **days** and **months**, and for the pronoun 'I'.

For example: *Morrissey, former lead singer of The Smiths, has recently released an album called 'You Are The Quarry'.*

Commas

A **comma** signals a pause within a sentence. It often separates one group of words in a sentence from another to keep the meaning of the sentence clear.

For example: *Although I was ill, I decided to go to work. However, I went home at lunchtime.*

Commas often appear as pairs (like brackets) when additional information is being provided.

For example: *Katy, whose work is normally very shoddy, made a special effort.*

Commas are also used to separate items in lists.

For example: *I bought eggs, bread, pasta, salad and milk.*

Remember: commas are not a substitute for full stops!

Task 6

The full stops are accurately positioned in the following items, but some commas would add control to the writing. Add commas where necessary.

1. He could resist everything but temptation and this was very tempting. However he had to think of an excuse.

2. Just at that moment I heard the car pull up outside and I knew I was in deep deep trouble. My parents who were returning from holiday would not be happy to see the empty cans of lager the crisp packets and the broken pots.

3. Duncan was only little but he noticed more than they thought. As the men moved the furniture he saw one of them slip a necklace into his pocket. Next the same man took a quick glance at a pair of Duncan's mother's earrings.

Question marks

A **question mark** replaces a full stop at the end of a sentence that is a question. For example:

Who is the President of the United States?

Would you please sign the cheque?

Task 7

Copy out these items, replacing full stops with question marks, if necessary.

1. What did he see in her. If he wasn't careful, she would have all his money. Would he come to his senses.

2. The question was worth asking. Where had he been at the time of the robbery. There was a doubt.

3. Wherever he went, the dog followed. The dog had adopted him. Would he adopt the dog.

Exclamation marks

An **exclamation mark** replaces a full stop at the end of a sentence that is an exclamation or a forceful command. For example:

What a fantastic match!

Don't touch that paint!

Task 8

Copy out these items, replacing full stops with exclamation marks, if necessary.

1. What a game. It was amazing.
2. Don't panic. In an emergency, keep calm.
3. He had never been to Africa before. He flew low over the desert. Unbelievable.

Speech marks

Speech marks are placed around the exact words spoken by someone (and quoted) in a piece of writing. For example:

After arriving late again, Gary said to Mick, 'I'll get the sack now.'

'Please sit down,' said Jamie, 'and enjoy the food.'

Task 9

Copy out the following items and add speech marks as required.

1. Queen Victoria said, We are not amused.
2. I wouldn't say I was the best manager in the business, said Brian Clough, but I was in the top one.
3. The boss pointed a playful finger at Lennie. He ain't much of a talker, is he?
    No, he ain't, but he's sure a hell of a good worker. Strong as a bull. Lennie smiled to himself. Strong as a bull, he repeated.

Spelling

'You're either good at spelling or you're not. There aren't any rules, so you can't learn how to spell.'

Correct spelling matters a lot – it is part of Standard English – and there are patterns to follow, whatever some people say. Maybe spelling in English is not easy, but it is BECAUSE English is international that the patterns are rich and varied...and therefore important to the language.

You do not need to be perfect at spelling, but you do need to be aware and alert. Start now to build an understanding of the patterns.

High-frequency words

High-frequency words are those words (less than 200 of them) that dominate our language, because they are the simple nuts-and-bolts words that hold sentences together.

Task 10

Find three spelling errors in each of the following sentences. Copy out the sentences, correcting the errors and highlighting the key words.

1. Rhys dose not like school, but he gose every day, becos he is the head teacher.
2. Sally took a apple for her teacher, but the teacher was not shure if it wass safe to eat it.
3. Do not make eny noise untill the frist bell rings.
4. She carnt swim o'r run whith her leg in plaster.
5. He whants to travel accross the wrold in a rowing boat.
6. We lent them are tent, and thay cept it for ages.
7. The plane took of eght hours late form Heathrow Airport.
8. He was onely five years old wen he whent to Oxford University.
9. I know understand who to drive an car.
10. Becky heared that she coud sing an dance on Broadway.

Homophones

Homophones are words that sound identical (or similar) to one another, but that are spelt differently.

Task 11

Here are some common homophones. Copy out the sentences carefully, filling the gap each time with the correct word. For extra emphasis, underline or highlight the key words.

1. **to too two**   The _____ sisters were _____ excited _____ eat their breakfast.
2. **it's its**   That cat of mine! _____ lucky to be alive. _____ head was stuck up a drainpipe.
3. **know no**   We _____ what the problem is, but so far _____ answer has been found.
4. **hear here**   I _____ that the Queen stayed _____ last week.
5. **write right**   He was naturally left-handed, but he learned to _____with his _____ hand.
6. **knew new**   We _____there would be trouble when the_____ boy arrived.
7. **who's whose**   _____ book is this? _____ is responsible for the damage?
8. **by buy**   He went to town _____ bus to _____ all his Christmas presents.
9. **where wear**   He did not know _____ the trousers were that he wanted to _____.
10. **passed past**   As he _____ the young people, he wondered where the _____ fifty years had gone.

Task 12

The following groups of words are mostly not precise homophones but, in practice, the way they are often pronounced leads to confusion in writing. Copy out the sentences, filling the gap each time with the correct word.

1. **where were we're** _____ all going on holiday to Tenerife. _____ are you going? You said you _____ going to Tenby.

2. **their there they're** _____ a disgrace. _____ behaviour is awful. _____ can be no excuse.

3. **of off 've** (have) I could _____ won a lot _____ money. I nearly fell _____ my chair at the thought.

4. **as has** _____ Lennie was so successful last year, he _____ been invited again this year. He _____ natural ability _____ a sword swallower.

5. **your you're** '_____ a handsome guy. _____ looks will be _____ fortune,' Gary said, looking at himself in the mirror.

6. **quite quiet** If you remain _____ for a few minutes, it is _____ likely that I will let you go on time.

7. **is his** _____ this really _____ work? _____ handwriting _____ different.

8. **lose loose** He is about to _____ a tooth. It is becoming _____.

9. **wary weary** After driving for so long, he was undoubtedly _____ . His passenger was _____ of him losing concentration.

10. **our are** _____ these _____ suitcases or do they belong to him?

Vowel choices

The sounds represented by different vowels and combinations of vowels vary. However, there are **groupings of words that work to the same pattern**, and it is not impossible to take in these groupings and patterns.

Task 13

Each of the following has an incorrect use of vowels. Write the correct spellings.

belive	speach	experiance	repare	feild
boaring	recieve	serius	injoyed	envolved
stedy	favorite	gaurd	usally	pritty
bilding	gilty	discribe	desease	coulor

Double consonants

Double consonants suffer from regular neglect. Sometimes doubles are required, and sometimes not.

Task 14

Double consonants are wrongly used, or missing, below. Write the correct spellings.

> Tommorow   dissapointed   dissapeared   proffesional
> toggether   ocassion   oposite   strugle   anoying   runing

Irregular plurals

The regular (and very common) way of forming an English plural is to add **s** to the singular noun, e.g. book → book**s**, dog → dog**s**.

Even most of the irregular plurals end in s. Most of the trouble lies in what happens <u>before</u> the **s**!

Some plurals end **–ies** (cities); some end **–es** (matches); some change from an **f** to a **v** and end **–ves** (leaves); and some seem as if they ought to belong to one of those groups but do not! (donkeys, beliefs).

Task 15

The plurals below show misunderstanding of spelling groups and patterns. Write the correct version of each word.

> countrys   charitys   familes   trollies   addreses
> monkys   boxes   centurys   thiefs   toyes

Word endings

Word endings are a very common area of spelling weakness. You need to be aware of groups and patterns again. For example, a group of words ends in **–le** (like 'artic**le**'), while another group ends in **–al** (like 'music**al**'). You need to check these out in your own work.

Task 16

Look out for familiar word endings and correct the following spellings.

> botherd   jumpt   takeing   handfull   happend   gratefull
> driveing   bullyed   breack   uncel   favourate   vehical
> sentance   regulary   beautifull   frightend   occasionly   finaly
> pleasent   unfortunatly   opend   probally   lonley   happyness
> anxios   audiable   sincerly   shakey   previos   opsion

Silent letters

Some silent letters have become silent over the centuries (e.g. de**b**t, clim**b**), while some just work to a pattern (e.g. the final silent **–e** in mate and bit**e**).

Task 17

In this task you have to insert the missing silent letter and/or adjust other letters.

> suttle   sighne   riting   weel   gost
> dett   climed   iland   sammon   nife

Polysyllabic words

These are the longer words, containing three or more syllables. In fact, breaking down such words into syllables is very useful in fixing on the correct spelling, e.g. *mul – ti – ply* (3 syllables).

Task 18

The following words are incorrectly spelt because of a misunderstanding of syllables.

> hoildays   tempory   misrable   buisness   rembering
> everthing   preformance   intresting   beging   devasting

EXTRAS

SPELLING

The above tasks should raise your awareness of the groups and patterns that are evident in English spelling. However, there is much more that you can do.

Concentrate on different categories of spelling, according to your personal weaknesses.

Build up groups of words that fit the same patterns. Find them in spelling lists, in textbooks of different school subjects, and in your own writing.

Other useful terms are:

Prefix – a syllable at the start of a word that changes the meaning of the word, e.g. **un**true, **dis**appear

Suffix – an extra part on the end of a word that creates another word, e.g. hope**ful**, hope**less**

Letter strings – a sequence of letters that occurs regularly, e.g. **str**ing, **str**uggle; en**ough**, thr**ough**

Grammar

'I speak English ok, so I don't need no grammar lessons. I write what I talk like.'

Standard English and agreement

Grammar is a set of rules for constructing sentences.

Standard English is spoken or written English that fits the accepted rules of grammar.

Agreement in grammar means matching the key words of a sentence in an acceptable way. For example, **we were**, not **we was**.

Task 19

Rewrite the sentences below in Standard English.

1. Mr Jenkins have been at the school for five years.
2. We digged the garden all day for a tenner each.
3. We was trying hard, but we was beat by half-time.
4. I always does my homework on the bus.
5. Jim lost it when he got the blame for summat he hadn't not done.
6. Him and me has been mates for yonks.
7. Them was the most bestest trainers in the shop.
8. Me and her have ate all the grub.
9. We done tons of work in English this afto.
10. I ain't done nothing and I ain't got no money on me.

THE BRAINWASH BOX

- Sentences – don't let them run on and on.
- Punctuation – full stops are the thing.
- Spelling – think of patterns.
- Grammar – remember you're writing, not speaking.
- Proof-read your writing – hunt down your own errors.

Get your basic skills in shape!

Answers to the questions in Unit 2.3 are in the *Teacher's Guide*.

Unit 3.1 — Searching and finding

LOCATING DETAILS

'If I copy out the right chunk, I'll get the marks.'

Looking for details in a text is one of the most basic reading skills. It is also one of the most important.

It is highly likely that one question on either a non-fiction or a media text will ask you to find five or 10 details. This requires you to read closely and select points efficiently. If you copy out a chunk of text thoughtlessly, you will only get a low score.

The search-and-find question is often (though not always) the first one in the section. It is possible to score the full 10 marks with a little bit of care. Don't throw marks away by only looking for a couple of details. Track the text patiently and select the key words and phrases.

The question will probably ask for your answer to be in a list.

Do not waste time repeating or explaining.

CHECKLIST ✔ **Locating details** means **finding things** in a text.
Search-and-find is another name for the same skill. It is also called **information retrieval**.
'**According to the text**' is a phrase often used in the question because it reminds you that the answers are 'facts' within the text.

The text

Read the following obituary of Max Schmeling, the former World Heavyweight Boxing Champion. The text is adapted from the website www.auschwitz.dk which pledges never to forget the victims and the heroes of the Holocaust.

Max Schmeling

Died 2 February 2005, aged 99

THE STORY OF A HERO

Max Schmeling, as World Heavyweight boxing champion from 1930 to 1932, was one of the best-known Germans from the Nazi era. He was sometimes seen as a willing model for Adolf Hitler's Aryan Superman. However, although he did have lunch with Hitler and had lengthy conversations with Goebbels, the master propagandist of the Nazi regime, his tale is far more complex than it first appears.

The story of Max Schmeling is the story of a hero, who during the Kristallnacht massacre of November 1938, saved the lives of two young Jewish brothers named Lewin. Schmeling was a decent man who was in conflict with the Nazi regime and who opposed the racial policies of Hitler's Third Reich. He showed extraordinary generosity and humanity. Yet he never once revealed his heroism…

Max Schmeling was a shy man of extremely humble origins who came of age amidst the glitter and turbulence of Berlin's 'Golden Twenties'. As the heavyweight champion of Europe, his career inevitably took him to America. Arriving in New York, he won the world title after victories over Johnny Risko and Jack Sharkey in 1930. He defended it the next year but lost it to Sharkey in '32 in a blatantly unfair decision. Four years later, he returned to America as the sacrificial lamb for the invincible Joe Louis. Although he was the underdog, Schmeling achieved what some consider to be the upset of the century by beating Louis.

Joe Louis won the rematch on 22 June 1938, in one of the most discussed fights of all time – and also one of the briefest. The fight was portrayed as the battle of the Aryan versus the Black, as the struggle of evil against good.

In a 1975 interview, Schmeling recalled the defeat: 'Looking back, I'm almost happy I lost that fight. Just imagine if

I would have come back to Germany with a victory. I had nothing to do with the Nazis, but they would have given me a medal. After the war I might have been considered a war criminal.'

During the '36 Olympics Max Schmeling gained a promise from Hitler that all US athletes would be protected. On several occasions Hitler tried to persuade the respected boxer into joining the Nazi Party, but Schemeling vigorously refused ever to join the Nazi Party or to publicize the Nazi propaganda line. Over Goebbels' personal protest, he refused to stop associating with German Jews or to fire his American Jewish manager, Joe Jacobs.

Two years later Schmeling agreed to hide the two teenage sons of a Jewish friend of his, David Lewin, during the awful time of Krystallnacht, November 1938, when Nazi attacks against the Jews reached new heights.

He kept the Lewin boys, Henry and Werner, in his apartment at the Excelsior Hotel in Berlin, leaving word at the desk that he was ill and no one was to visit him. Later, when the rage of hate died down a little bit, Schmeling helped them flee the country to safety. They escaped and came to the United States where one of them, Henry Lewin, became a prominent hotel owner. This episode remained a secret until 1989, when Henry Lewin invited Schmeling to Las Vegas to thank him for saving his life. To this day, Henry Lewin believes that he and his brother owe their lives to Max Schmeling and he is convinced that Schmeling himself could have died for his humanitarian gesture.

Hitler never forgave Schmeling for refusing to join the Nazi Party, so he had him drafted into the Paratroops and sent him on suicide missions.

After World War 2 Schmeling fought five times and, though he never made the top 10, he made enough money to purchase the Coca-Cola dealership. He was known as one of the most generous and charitable businessmen in Germany. Schmeling treasured loyalty and friendship and, somehow, each of his ring opponents became his friend. He regularly and quietly gave the down-and-out Joe Louis gifts of money, and the friendship continued after death: Schmeling paid for Louis' funeral.

Max Schmeling died on 2 February 2005 at the age of 99 at his home in Hollenstadt. His wife of 54 years, Ondra, died in 1987.

Schmeling became one of Germany's most respected sports figures, not only for his outstanding athletic accomplishments in the 1930s but for his humility, discipline and character.

The question

Now answer the following question:

- **List 10 points, according to the article, to show that Max Schmeling was not a Nazi.**

Try for the 10 marks

Before you study the sample answer, try to earn the 10 marks yourself:
- Focus on the key words of the question – **not a Nazi.**
- Go through the text methodically.
- Make each item as short as possible.
- Stick with the words of the text if they make the point clearly.
- Make more than 10 points if you can find them quickly.

The answer below therefore is probably the perfect answer to a 'list' question.

SAMPLE ANSWER

- He saved the lives of two Jewish brothers.
- He was in conflict with the Nazi regime.
- He opposed racial policies.
- He showed extraordinary generosity and humanity.
- 'I had nothing to do with the Nazis'.
- He gained a promise from Hitler that US athletes would be protected.
- He refused to join the Nazi Party.
- He refused to publicize the propaganda.
- He refused to stop associating with German Jews.
- He refused to fire his Jewish manager.
- He hid the two teenagers.
- He helped them flee the country.

COMMENT

The points come in clusters from paragraphs two, six and eight of the obituary. The writer returns to the tale of the two brothers in paragraphs seven and eight after mentioning it firstly in paragraph two. The sample answer is very successful because there is no fudging of the points in a long, unfocused answer. Write an answer like the one above and you will be the examiner's friend!

THE BRAINWASH BOX

- Make a list.
- Use bullet-points.
- Look for the full five or ten marks.

Change the question!

- a) **List five things the Nazis did to pressure Max Schmeling, according to the website obituary.**
  b) **List five things that Max Schmeling did to oppose the Nazis.**

EXTRAS

Location is at the heart of most of the harder reading skills: **selecting, highlighting, quoting, tracking the text** all depend on you being able to find things precisely.

Note:
- The first question of the section is not certain to be a 'List...' question.
- A 'search-and-find' question could ask you to find details in both texts, as a comparison question.

If the question says 'List...', use bullet-points and make a list!

Small picture, big picture

EXPLAINING AND SUMMARIZING

'It doesn't matter if you write waffle, because the examiners might not read it carefully.'

You need to be able to work out what is happening 'between the lines' in a non-fiction or media text. What attitude or what image does a text give to its readers? What purpose does the text have?

Can you select interesting and significant details and make probing comments about them? Can you explore and pinpoint the overall meaning of the text?

Explaining and summarizing call for careful 'joined-up' thinking – waffle will not work.

CHECKLIST ✔

> **Explaining** requires you to **use your own words to clarify** the meaning of some of the detailed content of a text.
>
> **Summarizing** means making clear and significant statements about **the meaning of the whole text.**
>
> An **attitude** is **a way of thinking and feeling** about something.
>
> An **image** can be the **general impression** that a person, organization or product gives to the public.
>
> The **purpose** of a text is the main thing that the text is **intended to achieve.** In non-fiction and media texts, the purpose is often to persuade the reader(s) to buy a product or agree with a point of view.

The text

Read the leaflet from the Hack Green Secret Nuclear Bunker in Cheshire, which is now an award-winning tourist attraction. (The 'outside' pages are on page 70, the 'inside' pages are on page 71.)

HACK GREEN SECRET NUCLEAR BUNKER

AS SEEN ON TV

PROTECT AND SURVIVE

ALERT STATE AMBER

AWARD WINNING

HOW TO FIND THE AWARD WINNING BUNKER

Located in the heart of the Cheshire countryside Hack Green Secret Nuclear Bunker is situated just off the A530 Whitchurch road, a few miles outside the picturesque market town of Nantwich, and only 30 minutes from Chester.

From junction 16 on the M6 motorway take the signs to Nantwich then to Whitchurch on the A530.
(Follow the Secret Bunker signs)

North West Tourist Board

TOURISM AWARDS 1999

HACK GREEN SECRET NUCLEAR BUNKER

- Wheelchair access to 1st floor and Bunker Bistro (reduced admission)
- Mother and baby facilities
- Facilities for the blind or partially sighted
- Facilities for deaf or hearing impaired

COME & GO AS YOU PLEASE YOUR ENTRY COVERS ALL THE FACILITIES ALL DAY.

The Bunker is open every day from the 3rd Saturday in March to the 31st October. 10.30 to 5.30. Winter openings, 11.00 to 4.30 every Saturday & Sunday, closed during December. Schools and groups are welcome at special rates.
Reserve a place on our special curator's evening tours a behind the scenes experience available all year round.
For latest details of opening times & admission prices, please ring the bunker information line:

01270 629219

Fax: 01270 629218
Email: coldwar@hackgreen.co.uk
Website: www.hackgreen.co.uk
P.O. Box 127, Nantwich, Cheshire CW5 8AQ

HACK GREEN SECRET NUCLEAR BUNKER

"A unique and exciting day out for all the family. Discovering history you can see, feel & touch"

"great fun for the kids"

"thank goodness it never had to be used"

- WWII Radar Station.
- Military vehicle collection
- Massive Operating Marconi Air Defence Radar
- B.M.E.W.S. (Ballistic, Missile, Early, Warning, System.) Operations room
- NEW! Real WE177 & Project Chevaline (Trident) strategic Thermonuclear Weapons
- NEW! The largest Early Warning R.A.F Shackleton model in the world

RADAR TECHNOLOGY

KIDS HAVE FUN TOO!

Follow the Soviet Spy Mouse Trail
Your SECRET mission is to find the enemy spy mice hidden in the bunker.

...what a fascinating day out...

we are looking forward to another visit

Did you Know?

"It is thought that in a nuclear war the UK would expect 200 megatons of nuclear weapons to be delivered against approximately 80 targets."
Central Office of Information 1980

"A surprise attack of which we would only get 4 minutes warning, whilst not impossible is considered unlikely"
Civil Defence Plan 1990

"It can be assumed that the population surviving an attack would range from 60% in primary targets to 95% in least damaged areas"
Home Defence Plan 1973

"the strategic stockpile of foodstuffs held for distribution to the popuation, post strike includes, flour, yeast, sugar, fat, biscuits, tinned meat and cake mix. In excess of 200,000 tons of goods are stockpiled".
M.A.F.F. 1995

DISCOVER THE SECRET WORLD OF NUCLEAR GOVERNMENT

For over 50 years this vast underground complex, remained secret, hidden on the outskirts of a sleepy Cheshire town. Declassified in 1993, the 35,000 sq ft underground bunker would have been the centre of Regional Government had nuclear war broken out.

Built in the 1950's as part of a vast secret radar network codenamed 'ROTOR'. The bunker today offers a warm welcome to anyone looking for a totally different day out. Entering through the massive blast doors, you will be transported into the chilling world of the Cold War. Re-built in the 1980's at a cost of over £32 million, it was transformed into the blastproof headquarters you can explore today. For the first time you can see the governments preparations for nuclear war and step into the lives of those who worked here. Minister of State's office, life support, communication centre, decontamination facilities, telephone exchange and much more! View original broadcasts to be transmitted on all TV channels prior to a nuclear attack. Tons of authentic equipment in original settings fire the imagination, with an exciting glimpse into England's dramatic Cold War past. Learn what living conditions were like, really getting to grips with the reality of the nuclear threat. Hear the sounds, even the smells of a working Civil Defence H.Q. at the height of the Cold War. Exciting real life operation rooms and many audio-visual presentations. Two superb cinemas showing previously secret films. Explore the labyrinth of spooky corridors. All the family will enjoy the Hands On activities. An all Weather Attraction, the bunker is a huge adventure playground in itself. Younger children can have bundles of fun as secret agents, following the Soviet Spy Mouse Trail. Before ending your eye-opening tour, visit the Bunker Bistro for your survival rations. And don't miss our shop, take home a souvenir of your visit to the secret world of nuclear government.

Above Ground
The massive re-enforced concrete bunker with 35 metre radio communications tower and air defence radar

Underground Level 1
Government headquarters, administration centre and technical departments

Underground Level 2
Communications centre, BBC studio, Scientists, Minister of State, Life support ect.

"Where history comes alive"

"...all this was going on only a few miles from our house!"

The question

Now answer the following question:

- What impressions do you get of the Hack Green Secret Nuclear Bunker from the leaflet?

Look at:
- what the leaflet says
- how the leaflet says it
- layout and illustrations.

Be selective

There is a lot of material on the leaflet and you need to work hard on selection of details. You should not read a leaflet like a short story – leaflets are designed to take your eyes initially in several directions. Close reading comes when you have taken in the overall message.

Before or after you have tried to write an answer yourself, read the sample answer below.

SAMPLE ANSWER

The impressions that the leaflet gives of the Hack Green Nuclear Bunker are that it is a cross between a museum and an activity centre. It tries to look like fun for the whole family and also it is obviously interesting for people who like history. But it's not a very attractive place or a very attractive topic, so they are trying to put a spin on it. They say it's a place 'where history comes alive' and there's a picture of a cloud of smoke on the front like a nuclear explosion!

The leaflet makes you feel that the bunker was very important and very secret. It tells you in detail about how it remained secret for over 50 years, it is underground and how it cost 32 million pounds to make it blast proof. It tells you the history in a way that world war fanatics would like.

It tells you about the different experiences you can have. You can 'learn what living conditions were like' and you can 'hear the sounds, even the smells'. Older people who went through the Cold War will think of that time. 'The chilling world of the Cold War.' It uses the words 'secret' and 'declassified' a lot which I find annoying, but I think they are there to impress people to try to convince them that it is exciting.

It shows it can be a lot of fun for children, 'Kids have fun too!', so there are some activities to do, especially a spy trail. It is saying that any kind of ages can go there. Not many places offer all these facilities for wheelchair access, mother and baby facilities, the blind or partially sighted, for the deaf or hearing impaired

The illustrations are very good, there is a sketch of the bunker and the two floors underneath. There are pictures of the rooms in working order too with people in them phoning and working like it would have been.

COMMENT

This answer selects a lot of details and makes quite a few sensible comments. It would be due a high mark and a clear C grade. Of course, there is plenty more that could be said and it could be better organized, but the coverage of the leaflet is good, the bullet-points have been used and, above all, the question has been thoroughly explored.

THE BRAINWASH BOX

- Write clear, controlled sentences explaining the text.
- Use your own words where possible to explain meanings.
- Focus on the key words of the question.

Change the question!

- **What kinds of people is the Hack Green Secret Nuclear Bunker leaflet aimed at? What evidence can you find to support your views?**

Consider:
- what the leaflet says
- how it says it
- the layout and pictures.

E**X**TRAS

Irony

If you thought there was something **odd** or even **amusing** about a nuclear bunker becoming a tourist attraction, you were probably seeing the **irony** of a **situation**. Think about it – a place associated with a potential nuclear holocaust becomes somewhere for kids to run around on a spy trail. Anybody is welcome in a top secret hideaway! Just pay your entrance fee!

Irony is all around us – it is a **twist** on the ordinary; it is the **unexpected**; often it is the very **opposite of the expected**.

You can have **tragic irony** or **comic irony** and many **subtle** variations in between. Look out for writers who do not quite mean what they say – their writing **tone** or **voice** uses **gentle irony** (associated with **wit** and **humour**) or **heavy irony** (close to **sarcasm**). There can be an accidental or deliberate **shift** as a text develops.

You do not need to be an expert on irony – you just need to read with your eyes and ears open! The sample answer on Hack Green began to show a sense of irony with the comment *'But it's not a very attractive place or a very attractive topic, so they are trying to put a spin on it.'*

Work hard on the reading – take care with your explaining.

ANALYSING PERSUASIVE TECHNIQUES

'They normally ask how something persuades you, and I normally say "It doesn't!"'

If you want to see how something works, you have to get inside it. If you want to find out **how** a piece of writing **tries to persuade** you, you have to read **below the surface**.

The writer tells you this, the writer tells you that, but how does she or he try to persuade you?

The writer may write positively or negatively, and could be putting across a point of view gently or aggressively. There may be the promise of a reward or bribe, but the writer might also be trying to scare you or make you feel sorry.

You may detect that the writer states some things firmly, but only hints at other things. He or she may take on the role of a collaborative friend, but may also mock and threaten you.

Treat the writer as clever, and be cautious as you read. Don't fall for the obvious. Look for hidden meanings.

CHECKLIST

> **Analysing** means **inspecting something in detail.**
>
> **Persuasive techniques** are the **skills and tricks** used by a writer to win the attention and support of a reader.
>
> The word **persuade** may be included in the question, but **tempt, encourage** and **convince** are used as alternatives.

The text

Read the letter sent to specially chosen members of the public by Incentives Unlimited.

INCENTIVES ⊕ UNLIMITED

CONGRATULATIONS.... **J Smith!**

If you've never won a big prize before, your efforts are finally being rewarded.

Today you've been awarded one of four fabulous prizes shown below.

CONFIRMED AWARD RECIPIENT:

Mr J Smith
The Cottage
The Street
Burnham Magna
Norfolk
NR63 0BM

95187

A Brand New Renault Clio 16V - the most popular small car in the UK.

Four-day, three-night Paris Coach Tour with accommodation and coach transport paid for.

£3,500.00 cash.... yours to spend any way you wish.

£2,200.00 worth of household appliances or furniture of your choice.

Here's great news for you, J Smith

Our research indicates that you have entered a number of prize draws, competitions or sweepstakes but, so far, you have never won a worthwhile prize. We are a public relations and promotions company, and we have been retained by the Sponsor to reward loyal participants like yourself.

To achieve this, <u>we have persuaded the Sponsor to allow us to give to you one of the items shown alongside FREE OF CHARGE</u>.... provided only that you claim it within 10 days and pay a nominal processing fee of only £6.95 to help cover delivery, handling and all applicable charges.

Please note, **Mr Smith** this is not a random prize draw or a competition. It is a <u>guaranteed</u> prize award to show the Sponsor's appreciation of your past participation. There are absolutely no strings attached other than your need to claim within 10 days and the nominal processing fee. Also, you are under no obligation whatsoever to buy anything - either now or in the future. And, if you do not wish to receive any more mail from us, simply let us know and we will ensure that your details are deleted from our list.

So do not delay! Complete your Prize Claim Voucher below and return it, in the envelope provided, with your claim fee right now.

Yours truly,

James R Cavendish

Awards Distribution Coordinator

P.S. It is my duty to warn you that, if you do not respond by the deadline, I have strict instructions to re-allocate the prize which has been reserved for you to someone else. So please send in your claim without delay!

▼ Detach along the dotted line ▼

Prize Claim Voucher

File No: 3033   Approval No: U35B011122

Please tick all applicable boxes:

❏ I confirm that I am the _____ J Smith _____ of the
address shown alongside and that I am over 18 years of age.

❏ I confirm having entered numerous draws but I have not yet won a
substantial prize.

❏ I wish to claim my prize as detailed above and confirmed by the official
terms and conditions overleaf.

❏ I enclose cheque/postal order for the nominal processing fee of £6.95
made payable to Incentives Unlimited.

❏ I have added an optional extra £3.05 for Express Processing.

Please charge my Credit Card:

Card No: _____   Exp Date: _____ / _____   Signature: _____

CONFIRMED AWARD RECIPIENT:

Mr J Smith
The Cottage
The Street
Burnham Magna
Norfolk
NR63 0BM

Your card will be debited by ISO

MAIN   UK-PR-TRV-ACQ-0035-CS
TRV005-1

Post in the envelope provided or plain white envelope to: Incentives Unlimited, PO Box 89, 61 Praed Street, Paddington, W2 1NS

The question

Now answer the following question:

- **How does the letter from Incentives Unlimited try to tempt you to 'claim a prize'?**

Think about:
- the heading
- the content
- the writer's choice of words
- the layout and illustrations.

Write an answer to the above question, before or after you have read the sample answer below. Don't forget to comment on the persuasive techniques used in the letter.

SAMPLE ANSWER

The writer tries to tempt you to claim a prize by making it all sound fantastic, for example 'there are absolutely no strings attached' and 'here's great news for you', and these are only two. Some words are emphasized by underlining them or writing them in bold. E.g. FREE OF CHARGE, guaranteed which tries to assure you that the prizes are genuine. It orders you to 'claim without delay'. The writer also uses pictures of some of the prizes available, and this would attract the reader's attention straightaway after seeing them, because they're all top prizes.

The writer also tries to tempt you by saying that if you don't wish to be contacted further then they will listen to you and not bother you anymore. That could maybe gain your trust and could also tempt you to claim your prize.

'Confirmed award recipient' makes people think that there is not a way it could be a fake because it says that they have definitely won a prize. The way it says 'you' in the sentence 'We have persuaded the sponsor to allow us to give 'you' one of the items...' makes people think they are the only ones who have won this special prize.

The main focus seems to be around getting you not to do what I would do (take a quick glance at it and say 'con-trick', then throw it in the bin) and to claim your prize. The writer tries to build up the tension all the way through and then by the end makes one last attempt to persuade you and then by the end you're thinking that you should claim it because it only costs just under £7 after all. The writer uses words like 'obligation' and 'participants' to make the letter sound professional and true, but in my opinion the letter is not true because I do not think companies would give all of these prizes away free of charge.

COMMENT

This answer shows a very clear understanding of the methods used by Incentives Unlimited to tempt the reader's natural curiosity. The student can barely resist an attack on the company, but does successfully keep the focus on how the persuasion is built up. This answer comfortably enters C grade.

THE BRAINWASH BOX

- Read the text, not just the headline and picture.
- Pick out interesting features.
- Avoid vague comments.
- Look for persuasive words and phrases and comment on them.

Change the question!

- **What image is created of Incentives Unlimited, the company that has sent this letter?**

Consider:
- The content of the letter
- The language used
- The layout and pictures.

EXTRAS

Emotive language is language that arouses feelings (emotions) – words, phrases or sentences that produce shock, anger, excitement, pride, etc.

A **connotation** is a **suggested meaning** of a word or phrase; a **denotation** is an **actual meaning**. For example, 'elderly' and 'senile' both denote 'old', but they suggest different conditions – they have different connotations.

Persuasive and **emotive language** can be associated with **overstatement** and **exaggeration** and **superlatives**, all of which are regularly part of **advertising 'hype'**, where someone is trying to 'sell' you a product or an idea.

When something is **understated**, it is often being described or expressed in a **subtle, more modest, way**.

Emotive language is **not neutral**. It is 'outside the norm'. Be alert for words, phrases and sentences that appear in a text to **create a special effect**.

Don't settle for 'The writer says...'.

Unit 3.4 — Black, white, and shades of grey

COMPARING NON-FICTION AND MEDIA TEXTS

'One of them usually has a big, black and bold headline ... and the other one doesn't!'

The comparison question demands a **well-organized** response. You will be asked to explore two texts and possibly four bullet-points for a 10-mark question. It stands to reason that you will be more successful if you take the question coolly. Therefore, go steadily through your answer in a measured, not a rushed, way.

Once again, avoid vague points. If the comment you make can be applied to any media text from any previous exams, it cannot be worth much. A news headline, for example, comes with the type of writing and you would expect an article or report to have one. It is what you can say about the particular headline that counts. Write about the items in front of you, not any old texts.

Cross-referencing is a difficult skill – take care with your comments. Look carefully at the key words in the question:
- ...similarities and differences
- Compare and contrast...
- ...more effective...
- ...more impact...
- ...your impressions from the two texts...

Be alert to other forms of comparison questions too.

CHECKLIST ✓ **Cross-referencing** is a **link** made between one text and another.

Similarities and differences refer to details that are alike in two texts and things that are not alike. **Compare and contrast** also suggests something very close to similarities and differences, though **contrast** suggests something that is STRIKINGLY different or even opposite.

A question with **more effective** or **more impact** in it is asking you to **judge** or **evaluate** which of the texts is better at what it is trying to achieve – **its purpose.**

The text

Read the texts on the next four pages: a leaflet promoting Kip McGrath Education Centres and an article written by a parent and published on the BBC Education website.

So what can you expect from Kip McGrath?

Firstly, we carry out a free assessment to establish your child's needs. We discuss this confidentially with you, and explain how we can maximise the strengths and address the weaknesses. If there's no problem – we tell you.

Secondly, we create a personal workplan especially for your child. This enables us to set challenging but attainable goals, and to continually re-assess performance throughout the term. At his or her own pace, your child's success is personal and individual.

Thirdly, we keep you informed. You'll see improvement yourself, and our Centre Director is usually available for an informal chat – but sometimes a formal appointment may be necessary.

Our pledge to you

- Your child will be treated in a way that won't frighten or embarrass
- We will strive to make learning a stimulating activity, not a chore
- The centre will promote high standards of respect and courtesy
- Effort will be valued and rewarded as highly as achievement
- Our tutors will always offer you friendly help and advice

English

Reading, Writing, Spelling, Grammar, Creative Writing, Comprehension, Vocabulary Development.

Mathematics

Basic Number Skills, Mental Calculations, Tables, Fractions, Decimals, Percentages, Algebra, Geometry, Problem Solving

Many children experience difficulty with mathematics at some point, either early on in Year 2 or as complex concepts are introduced in Years 7 or 8. Often, with professional assessment, the cause emerges as a misunderstanding of basic principles.

In English, too, some children will struggle with reading and writing as a whole or with key elements such as spelling or grammar. As a first language or second, not everyone is born with an ability in the subject; and individual problems can be addressed.

Many parents worry about how their children perform in these critical subjects, so at Kip McGrath our professional tutors are trained in exactly these areas. We'll find the cause of the trouble, and then create a workplan to address the main issues.

We have over 25 years experience helping children rekindle motivation, renew self-esteem and find the way to better exam results. Children do not merely learn and succeed, they learn to succeed; a skill that often helps performance in other subjects.

Give your child a brighter future and give yourself peace of mind

Kip McGrath is the cool way to top-up the school day!

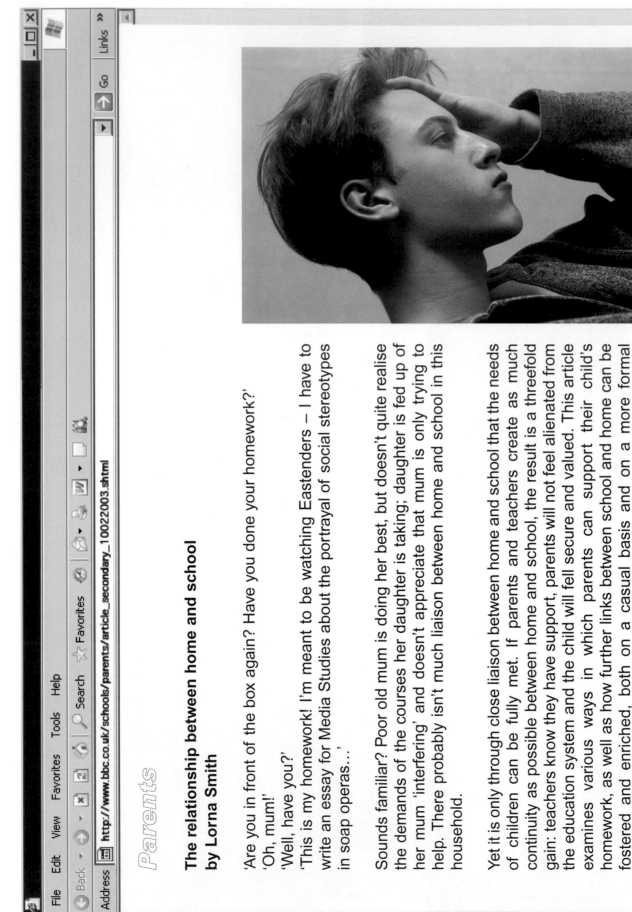

Address http://www.bbc.co.uk/schools/parents/article_secondary_10022003.shtml

Parents

**The relationship between home and school
by Lorna Smith**

'Are you in front of the box again? Have you done your homework?'

'Oh, mum!'

'Well, have you?'

'This is my homework! I'm meant to be watching Eastenders – I have to write an essay for Media Studies about the portrayal of social stereotypes in soap operas...'

Sounds familiar? Poor old mum is doing her best, but doesn't quite realise the demands of the courses her daughter is taking; daughter is fed up of her mum 'interfering' and doesn't appreciate that mum is only trying to help. There probably isn't much liaison between home and school in this household.

Yet it is only through close liaison between home and school that the needs of children can be fully met. If parents and teachers create as much continuity as possible between home and school, the result is a threefold gain: teachers know they have support, parents will not feel alienated from the education system and the child will fell secure and valued. This article examines various ways in which parents can support their child's homework, as well as how further links between school and home can be fostered and enriched, both on a casual basis and on a more formal footing.

Homework

- Check your child's homework diary on a regular basis. Many schools run a system whereby parents are asked to sign the homework diary every week, which is countersigned by the tutor. There is often a space for a written comment too; so this is an opportunity for a simple exchange of information.
- Ensure that your child does their homework. This is, of course, not necessarily an easy thing to do, but you can help by showing a genuine interest in what they are studying.
- Make sure that your child has a place to work that is uncluttered and as quiet as possible – even if that means suggesting they work at the local library or a grandparent's house a few times a week.
- Pin up their homework timetable so that you are aware of what should be set.
- Check that they are working for roughly the right amount of time. Schools usually have guidelines that state the amount of work a child should be set per night. Contact the school if your child appears to be getting too much or too little.
- Discuss with your child the best time to do the homework. Some prefer to get it out of the way straight from school, others need a chance to relax between putting down a pen and picking it up again.
- Encourage your child to take regular short breaks.
- Keep TV as a treat for when they have completed a certain task.
- Try to be on hand to go over spellings or other topics on which your child might be tested.
- Suggest that your child does the major part of a piece of homework (like writing an essay) on one night, then comes back to it briefly the following night to check it through, when they are fresh.

Other things you can help with from home:

- Put a copy of your child's timetable up in the kitchen so that you can help them prepare for school each day. Pack their bag with them the night before and ensure they have the necessary equipment for the day ahead, including a PE kit if necessary.
- Try to find a regular time to talk with your child about their school day. With younger children, you may be able to hear them read and comment on their progress in a notebook.
- Make sure that you are receiving letters from school. Check whether there is a set day on which letters go home.
- Do notify the school as soon as possible if your child will not be present. A phone message followed up with a brief written note is usually best.

The question

Now answer the following question:

- Both the leaflet and the Internet article are about the importance of taking your education seriously.
  Compare the two, saying which you find more effective, and why.

You will need to compare each of the following separately:
- content and message
- pictures or illustrations
- overall presentation
- the writers' choice of words.

Make your case

In a question like this, the choice is 'free'. You can write **in favour of either text**, but you must **refer properly to both texts**. You do not have to take an absolute view – one is good, the other bad – you can reflect instead on the strengths and weaknesses of both. In the end though, do not duck the decision. Make the case and win the argument.

SAMPLE ANSWER

The leaflet offers us places children can go to improve their studies, while the Internet article says what parents can do at home to ensure that their children get on with their studies. I think the leaflet is more effective than the Internet article.

The Internet article in my opinion contains too much information and repeats itself, though the advice to parents is written in bullet points which is good. The content in the Internet article is very boring, it tells parents how to treat their children when they're doing homework. It uses a dialogue to show a situation, then it gives some ideas. The message it gives out is that parents need to be more involved in their childrens education and it tells them how. The content of the leaflet is well laid out and is very clear and simple. The leaflet gives a lot of facts about the way children learn and problems they may have. It offers help and advice, and it reassures parents and children in a very friendly way. It tells you step by step what you can expect from Kip McGrath and it makes a pledge to everybody. It refers to "Personal, professional tutoring in English and Maths." This makes the parent feel that it is a proper, experienced teacher but it is not like school. It says about having lessons once a week which would be more practical than the article which suggests parents watch their children's homework. It tells parents to "Give yourself peace of mind."

The picture in the internet article is of a teenage boy concentrating on his homework, looking bored. The pictures in the leaflet are colourful and would attract parents because the children in the pictures are enjoying learning there. They show boys and girls of all ages.

In the Internet article, the writer starts off with a conversation between a mother and child talking about homework, a normal row about whether the child has completed or not. This seems familiar to the parent and makes them feel better, because it will make them feel they haven't done anything wrong. But it isn't really practical and the children would find a way around the parents. In the leaflet they suggest professional tutoring which is more beneficial for the children and they can learn from a teacher.

COMMENT

The student has done quite well here, coping with the two texts, both of them containing a lot of reading material. She or he keeps everything clearly referenced – leaflet and article – and achieves a reasonable balance, while clearly supporting one of the texts, the leaflet. There could be much closer work on language (the choices of particular words and phrases), but the organization, clarity, control and length earns this a C grade mark.

THE BRAINWASH BOX

- Look for the focus of the question.
- Use the bullet-points in the question to structure your answer.
- Don't get in a muddle between the two texts.
- Don't write too much.

Change the question!

- The leaflet and the Internet article are both about out-of-school study for school pupils.
  Compare and contrast the two texts.

Consider in each text:
- purpose
- audience
- content and message
- particular words and phrases
- layout, headings and pictures.

EXTRAS

Certain **connectives** (words that link sentences) and **conjunctions** (words that link within sentences) work well in comparison questions.

Try using the following:

...whereas...   ...while...   ...although...   ...but...   ...however,...
In contrast,...   In comparison,...

The conjunctions in the first line can appear at the start of sentences or in the middle.

The connectives in the second line appear at the start of the sentence, immediately followed by a comma.

Keep your comparison response clearly and logically organized.

Unit 4.1

Aiming straight

TRANSACTIONAL WRITING

'They ask your opinion about something – so I give them a piece of my mind!'

Transactional writing is 'real-life' writing with a clear direction from the writer to the reader. At its simplest, it may mean a note for the milkman 'No milk today, thanks' or a road-sign 'Delays ahead'. Both of these involve a clear transaction (or a communication) – the first of them from the customer to the milkman, the second of them from the traffic controllers to the motorists.

Unfortunately, you will not be asked to do communication tasks quite as simple as the ones above! In extended transactional tasks, you will be expected to offer a considered opinion on a topic, and you will have to **argue** or **persuade** or **advise** (or maybe all three!)

You may be asked to write a **letter**, a **formal report**, a **speech** or a **leaflet**. They are all explained in this unit. You could also be asked to write a magazine or newspaper article, which are covered in the following unit on discursive writing. Transactional writing overlaps with discursive writing.

The key questions to ask when doing a transactional piece of writing are:
- What is the **purpose**? (i.e. the reason for the task).
- Who is the **audience**? (i.e. the person or people reading it).
- What is the **format**? (i.e. the shape and layout of the writing).

In each part of this unit there is an opening to a sample answer. Use the opening and continue the answer in each case.

Letter writing

CHECKLIST

> ### LETTERS
>
> A **letter** can be **informal** (relaxed) or **formal** (official business). You would expect on all letters to see the **sender's address on the top right** of the page, with the **date** immediately below. If the letter is formal, the receiver's address should be on the left. **Dear Sir/Madam** matches **Yours faithfully** in very formal letters. **Yours sincerely** is acceptable as a semi-formal sign-off for most letters. Informal letters can end with **All the best** or any other friendly parting.

The question

Consider the following task:

- Your local council has just issued a polite advice sheet to dog owners reminding them of their responsibilities and the problems of dogs in the community.

Write a letter to your local newspaper either criticizing or defending dog owners.

SAMPLE OPENING

> 31 Church Street
> Queenstown
> Berkshire
>
> 3rd February 2005
>
>
> The Editor
> Berkshire Telegraph
> Market Place
> Queenstown
>
> Dear Editor
>   I have to comment on the council's recent advice sheet to dog owners in the area…

Continue...

• Sense of **purpose**	Undecided (dog lover or not?).
• Sense of **audience**	Promising (formal, polite).
• **Format**	No errors (addresses and date).

Change the question!

- Imagine you have relatives living abroad. You have not been in touch for some time but you would like to visit them as it would be a cheap holiday.

  Write a letter which would persuade your relatives to agree to your visit. Remember to set the letter out appropriately.

Formal report writing

CHECKLIST ✔ **REPORTS**

A **formal report** is an official document normally written to someone in authority. It may be written by someone who is a **representative** for a group of people.

There should be a **full title** explaining the reason for the report and there should be a **date**.

The **name of the person writing the report** and the **person(s) receiving it** should be included.

Sub-headings are often used in reports, and **bullet-points** also appear, especially when there is a **list of recommendations** at the end of the report.

The question

Consider the following task:

- Your school is keen to improve the fitness levels of its pupils. It intends to have a 'fitness drive' for all year groups. The Headteacher has asked you, as the representative for Year 11, to write a report for the year group, suggesting how a 'fitness drive' would work best.

  Write the report for the Headteacher on behalf of Year 11.

Read the opening to a sample answer, then continue and complete the task.

SAMPLE OPENING

> ## Report on Ideas for a Fitness Drive for Year 11
>
> By: J_____ S_____   Year 11 Rep   To: Headteacher
>
> The purpose of this report is to underline the problems regarding the sport in this school...

Continue...

• *Sense of* **purpose**	Sport, not Fitness?
• *Sense of* **audience**	OK, but might get too critical?
• **Format**	So far, so good. Sub-headings?

Change the question!

- Your town or district has received a grant to improve local facilities. **Write a report to the local council suggesting how this money could be spent to benefit the community.**

Think about: purpose (suggest ideas), audience (local council), and format (report).

Speech writing

CHECKLIST

> ✓ **SPEECHES AND CONTRIBUTIONS TO RADIO PROGRAMMES**
>
> In most cases, a 'speech' should **begin without fuss**. There is no need for 'Ladies and gentlemen...' etc.
>
> Do not start a phone-in contribution with a dialogue with the presenter or a tribute to the quality of the programme!
>
> Write in **full sentences** because you are **arguing a case**. Notes are not enough. **Paragraphs** will show a **sense of order**, but there are **no other requirements** of format.
>
> You will be arguing from a personal point of view.

The question

Consider the following task:

- The 2012 Olympic Games will be staged in London. Many people support the idea, but many others think that the Government's money should not be spent on London and the Olympics.
  A radio station is running a phone-in on this topic and you decide to contribute. You know that you will have limited time on air and you need to organize your thoughts, so you prepare yourself by writing down what you want to say.
  Write your contribution to the radio programme.

SAMPLE OPENING

> Hi Simon, I'm not a Londoner, but I think it will be great for this country to hold the Olympics during my lifetime...

Continue...

- *Sense of **purpose***   We know where he stands!
- *Sense of **audience***   Relaxed, not too formal.
- ***Format***   Quick hello, then straight to it.

Change the question!

- A debate is being held in your class on vegetarianism. You have to make a speech either for or against.
  Write what you would say.

Think about: purpose (persuade for or against vegetarianism), audience (your classmates), and format (speech).

Leaflet writing

CHECKLIST   **LEAFLETS**

A **leaflet** should have a **heading** and **sub-headings**.

Use **bullet-points** (but do not overdo them).

You can write in **columns**, but you do not have to.

Do not draw a picture – just draw the box.

The question

Consider the following task:

- 'Experts say that binge-drinking is a bigger problem among young people than drug abuse.'
  Write a leaflet, aimed particularly at teenagers, to discourage them from 'binge-drinking'.

SAMPLE OPENING

> ## BE SELFISH – LOOK AFTER NO. 1 – DON'T BINGE!
>
> *Binge Drinking Is Bigger Than Drugs*
>
> *Are you one of those people who follow the crowd?...*

Continue...

• *Sense of **purpose***	Well on task with clever heading.
• *Sense of **audience***	Strongly directed at teenagers.
• ***Format***	Might be article, not leaflet, but it's good.

Change the question!

- Your local junior school has invited you to produce a leaflet about road safety, aimed at 10- and 11-year-olds. It should be informative and persuasive. Think about ways of getting your message across clearly. You may want to show where illustrations would be included in your leaflet, but you should not spend time giving details of these.
  Write your leaflet.

Think about: purpose (to inform and persuade about road safety), audience (10- and 11-year-olds), and format (leaflet).

THE BRAINWASH BOX

- Argue a case.
- Win the argument.
- Be accurate.

EXTRAS

The types of writing covered in this unit all require some degree of **formal style**, following the **rules of Standard English**. Avoid slang!

In some cases, for example in a **report** or **formal letter**, you should avoid contracted (shortened) forms, e.g. *don't, I'm, there's*. Write *do not, I am, there is*. That is an easy way to give an impression of a more formal style.

Clear, sensible expression is always the top priority. Don't go out of your depth with fancy language!

Purpose, audience, format – but plan your ideas too!

Going public

DISCURSIVE WRITING

'I always do it in columns – I think they're impressed by that.'

There is a large overlap between discursive and transactional writing. Transactional writing tasks – including letters, speeches, formal reports and leaflets – often require you to **argue, persuade, advise**. Discursive writing tasks often require you to **analyse, review, comment**. In other words, you need to give opinions, backed up with detailed evidence. It will be clear to most people that the two sets of 'triplets' have a lot in common.

Discursive writing traditionally means 'essay' writing, where the rules can be quite strict and you have to write in a balanced way with a formal style. (To some extent this is still true in English literature essay writing.) Nowadays, however, in the world of journalism, discursive essays are better known as **articles** and **reviews**. This means that there is another link with transactional writing, because discursive writing also needs you to be aware of **purpose, audience** and **format**. Remember that this means you have to keep in mind **why you are writing, who you are writing for** and **the shape or structure** of your text.

Article and review writing

CHECKLIST

ARTICLES AND REVIEWS

A **newspaper or magazine article** is a piece of extended writing that **discusses a topic** that is relevant or interesting to its readers.

It is therefore quite important that the article is **lively** and fairly **committed** to the topic. An article is not the same as a newspaper report, which tends to be more 'eye-witness' and/or factual. An article may **discuss, on reflection, the issues** of the stories that have been in the news.

> A **review** is a type of article in which the writer **gives** his or her **considered opinion** of a new book, film, music, television, etc. Sometimes a review **looks back on a topic over a fixed period** of time, e.g. a review of the football season or the Athens Olympics.

The question

Consider the following task:

- You are asked to write a lively article for an American travel magazine, persuading Americans to have a holiday in Britain. You may concentrate on one particular area of Britain or the country as a whole.
  Write the magazine article.

SAMPLE OPENING

COME TO BRITAIN – OLD FRIENDS, NEW ATTRACTIONS!

Are you ready for a change from the Wild West and the skyscrapers and the Superbowl?
Have you been to Britain recently where the old and the new wait to entertain you?

Continue...

• Sense of **purpose**	Tempting readers to visit Britain, yes.
• Sense of **audience**	Targeting Americans, yes.
• **Format**	Lively headline, confidently done (you don't need to write in columns).

Change the question!

- A national newspaper is attempting to educate its older readers in the ways of the young. It needs up-to-date, lively articles on hobbies and interests – from fashion to football, from music to model-making, from computers to cars, from TV to tai-kwando.
  Write a lively article for the national newspaper on what is happening in your hobby or interest.

THE BRAINWASH **BOX**

- Be topical.
- Be enthusiastic.
- Be interesting.
- Be accurate.
- Avoid vague comments.

E✗TRAS

Register is another word for the **style**, **tone** or **voice** of a piece of writing. It becomes quite crucial in transactional and discursive writing.

When writing an article, the obvious distinctions are between adults, teenagers and children as different kinds of reader. But whatever the age and definition of the target readers (audience), there are still other choices to be made by the writer of an article.

You can, for example, write in a **clear**, **direct way**, going straight to the point. You can, however, be **deliberately puzzling** and tease your reader by holding back the real purpose of your article.

The tone that you choose can be fairly **formal and serious** OR it can be **chatty and informal**. There are many other varieties too – loud and brash, apologetic, expert, etc. – some of them subtle and changing, others very UN-subtle!

Give your discursive writing a sense of purpose and audience – do it for real!

Unit 4.3 Shame about the English...

TECHNICAL ACCURACY

Sentences and punctuation

'I use a comma if I need to breathe ...'

Don't trip yourself up in the exam by making lots of daft mistakes. Control what you write. Write – don't scribble.

CHECKLIST ✔ The key ideas for controlling your writing are as follows:

Know how to use **simple sentences, compound sentences** and **complex sentences.**

Use **full stops** consistently at the end of all of those sentence types.

Nice speech...shame about the punctuation!

Task 1

Punctuate the following with full stops only.

> (paragraph 1)
> Hi I'm phoning up about the topic of smoking in public I have very mixed feelings about this topic firstly I'm a non-smoker myself but it doesn't really bother me whether or not someone around me is smoking apart from when I'm in restaurants then the smoke really gets to me I hate it when you're going to sit down to have a meal when the people on the table behind you start to smoke it really puts you off surely they can wait until they've gone or have the decency to get up and go and smoke outside.

(paragraph 2)

Another thing I hate about smoking in public is when someone gets on the public transport and begins to smoke when there are plenty of signs up to inform them that there is no smoking on the transport but these ignorant people choose to ignore the signs and do exactly the opposite surely they could have had a cigarette before they got on the bus or wait a few minutes until they get off.

(paragraph 3)

I don't mind people smoking they know the health risks and are willing to take the risk so if they want to go around killing themselves let them just have the decency not to go around killing other people by passive smoking.

Now add commas to the three paragraphs.

EXTRAS

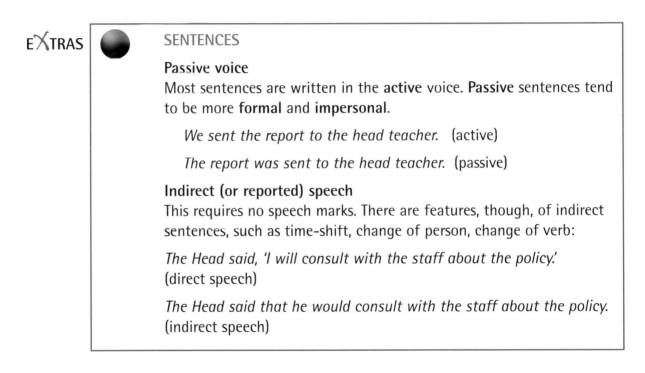

SENTENCES

Passive voice

Most sentences are written in the **active** voice. **Passive** sentences tend to be more **formal** and **impersonal**.

We sent the report to the head teacher. (active)

The report was sent to the head teacher. (passive)

Indirect (or reported) speech

This requires no speech marks. There are features, though, of indirect sentences, such as time-shift, change of person, change of verb:

The Head said, 'I will consult with the staff about the policy.' (direct speech)

The Head said that he would consult with the staff about the policy. (indirect speech)

EXTRAS

> **PUNCTUATION**
>
> **Apostrophes** (') are used when there are **shortened forms of words**. The apostrophe usually replaces the missing letters:
>
> | | |
> |---|---|
> | do not > **don't** | I am > **I'm** |
> | they are > **they're** | would have > **would've** |
>
> Apostrophes are also used for **'ownership'** or **'belonging'**:
>
> | | |
> |---|---|
> | United**'s** manager | the band**'s** latest album |
> | the boxer**'s** black eyes | (one boxer only) |
> | the **boxers'** black eyes | (two or more boxers) |
>
> **Semi-colons** (;) can be used to separate two very closely linked sentences.
>
> *Wenger and Ferguson were rivals; they argued often.*
>
> **Colons** (:) show that something is to follow, often a list.
>
> *She had worked in several countries: Iraq, Iran, Turkey and Egypt.*
>
> **Brackets** are always used in pairs. They enclose information that is not part of the main meaning of the sentence. Pairs of commas and pairs of dashes can be used for the same purpose.
>
> *John Peel (1939–2004) was the most influential disc jockey ever.*

Paragraphs

Paragraphs are a very important part of organization. They are, in effect, another item of punctuation. Present your work in properly indented paragraphs of even length.

A paragraph should start with a key sentence, called a **topic sentence**.

Paragraphs give shape to a piece of writing and help the reader's eyes move around the page easily.

Nice letter...shame about the paragraphs!

Task 2

Decide where the paragraphs should start and finish in the following letter. There are **seven** paragraphs in the original letter, all properly indented. Copy out the opening (**topic**) sentences to the seven paragraphs.

95 Brush Street
Howton
England

17/08/05

The Editor
Daily Star Newspaper
London
WC1 3EE

Dear Sir/Madam,

I am writing to you in response to the letter you printed in Thursday's paper sent in by Mr Newebee! I feel this point of view is totally uncalled for and he does not deserve to have his letter printed. Pop stars, sports men and women, actors and actresses earn that kind of money because they actually do earn it. They are always working hard to perform the best they can and will pay the price for their fame. They will usually receive much unwanted press and criticism for what they do in and out of work. They usually have busy schedules and are especially working non-stop for very long periods of time. An example would be Jackie Chan who is fully booked right up to 2007 and he only earns half of what others earn. Don't you think he deserves reparation for his work? Movie stars and other famous positions that command high salaries do not just jump on the ride. They have to make themselves what they are and usually people actually pay to see them and become their fans. You see people actually make movies stars etc. What they are and if they like their work, people will see it/them and this will make their bosses money for which they will reward the star. Not all stars actually earn all that much. Some will rise and some will fall, but the majority in the business will hardly earn anything. This is down to the pessimistic view of the public. So stop complaining about the stars just grabbing money. They deserve what they get. Stars work hard to get where they are and even harder to stay there. You don't complain when an athlete wins gold for England, but you complain about the money they get. You are very irate about the way you think and act, which can be very annoying. You also know that most stars will attend charity events and usually donate money to good causes. An example of this is Elton John. Look what he does, probably more than you do and he earns a lot too, but he gives 25% to charity, so is he deserving of his fees? In short, you must agree that the stars push their way to the top and through hardships to get where they are today and I commend them and think they deserve every single penny they get. I ask that you (The Daily Star) print this letter to voice my views and opinions against the other letter. Thank-you for your time.

Yours sincerely,

(xxxxx xxxxxx)

Spelling and vocabulary

'If I keep my words simple, I don't make so many spelling mistakes.'

Always use the best words you can think of. Don't dumb down your choice of words just to avoid spelling mistakes BUT do take care with spelling, and avoid daft slips.

Nice leaflet...shame about the spelling!

Task 3

Find 20 spelling errors in this piece of writing.

STOP SMOKING NOW!!

This leaflet is specifically designed to target teenage smokers and try to encourage them to stop. Contained in this leaflett is help and advise on how to stop smoking for good.

   (*An illustration of a teanager smoking with a red cross threw*)

Why start smoking? It's not big and certainly dosn't look good. Today more and more youngsters are starting to smoke each day and usualy the main reasons why are:

   "My friends all do it so why can't I?"
   "It makes me look good."
   "My freinds will think I am borring if I don't join in."

These tend to be the main raisons why most poeple do start to smoke. Well their all wrong! All smoking does for you is:
1.   Increese the risk of lung cancer and heart desease.
2.   Puts tobacco toxins such as nicotine and carbon monoxide into your body.
3.   Take away your sence of taste, make your fingers go yellow and make your breath smell.
Also
Your general heath and fitness levells will drop.

All of these things can be sorted out over a number of years if you
STOP SMOKING NOW!

SO YOU WANT TO KNOW HOW!

1. Tell somone you are going to stop so they can help you aviod temtation.
2. Get rid of all of your cigarettes, matches and lighters. Also make a list of all of the good points an bad points of smoking to see for yourself how bad it is.
3. Take up a hobbie to take youre mind off things, like aerobics or knitting.
4. If you feel the urge to smoke try chewing gum or something else to take your mind of things.
5. Once you have started stick to it, think of all the good points at the end of it.

FOR MORE HELP AND ADVICE CALL:

WALES – 01222 641888   ENGLAND – 0171 4873000
(Picture of a fit and healthy teenager)

Nice report...shame about the slang!

One of the most difficult things in an exam is to choose your words carefully. Just try to be aware of the need to write Standard English, even formal (or posh!) English.

Task 4

Read the report on Energy Saving and make it more formal. You could:
* remove the references to 'I' and 'we'
* change some words and phrases
* change the punctuation and sentences.

REPORT TO SCHOOL GOVERNORS ON ENERGY SAVING
BY STUDENT REPRESENTATIVE

SAVING RESOURCES

As caring pupils of this school we are all a little fed up about the effects the school has on the local environment. So we have come up with this report to show ways in which us as a school can change the effects of wasting resources in the classrooms, and around the buildings.

SAVING WATER:

I am sure as a school we must waste loads of water each week from misuse. To try and cut down on the wastage of water we have come up with a few pointers which could save valuable resources.

1. Make sure all taps are fully turned off after use.
2. Only use water when necessary and don't waste it.

Just using these two simple things could cut wastages down by a little bit.

SAVING HEAT:

Again heat is lost daily from the school from simple things like leaving doors open. To try and reduce the loss we have come up with a few things which can be applied.

1. Close all doors after you, inside and out
2. Only use heaters when weather is freezing.
3. Reduce the amount of heat lost through doors by fitting draught excluders.
4. Fit double glazing in all rooms.

The last 2 points (3 and 4) would cost the school a bit of money but over the years that money could be made back over the reduced heating bill.

SAVING ENERGY:

This has to be the worst way of wasting resources of all, we are constantly wasting electricity on simple things around the school. Ways to reduce this are:

1. Make sure you only use the lights when needed.
2. Switch all lights and electrical stuff off after use.
3. Use those energy saving light bulbs instead of normal ones.

LITTER:

The area around us is constantly covered in litter, each day more and more gets dropped and thrown about the place, this also happens in school as well. To reduce this we could:

1. Introduce more litter bins in the schools grounds.
2. As punishment for chucking litter or any other offence pupils could be made to pick up the rubbish off the school grounds.

Point 2 not only would make them think twice about doing it again but would save wasting paper with lines or energy with detentions.

If all of these things were put into action I am sure it would make at least a small difference to the environment.

Other ways: Recycling products, ozone friendly products.

Grammar

'I don't go to a grammar school ...'

Grammar is the nuts and bolts of the language. If you do not apply some of the basic rules of grammar, you suggest you are low on skills. Stop now to read the points in the following checklist. Remember them and you will avoid some of the most obvious mistakes.

CHECKLIST ✓

Pronouns: These are the short words that replace nouns and are often used loosely. For example, **they** and **them** sometimes refer back to nothing in particular.

Comparatives and superlatives: Slack use of **better** and **best** (and others) is common. **Better** compares two items; **best** is the top item in a list of three or more. For example: *Arsenal are very good, Chelsea are even better, but the best team are _____!*

Prepositions are the short grammatical words that give a precise **position** or **direction** to a sentence. For example, you apply **for** a job, but you apply **to** a company.

Agreement is really the correct lining up of verbs in a sentence. **We were...** and **I was...** are both correct! Anything else isn't!

Verbs are at the heart of any sentence and, needless to say perhaps, plenty can go wrong with them when you are writing. Watch out for wrong **verb forms** in your work, e.g. **digged** instead of **dug**, and keep alert for incorrect changes of verb tenses – past, present and future.

Nice article...shame about the English!

So much can go wrong with a piece of writing. It must be the hardest thing anyone has to do in an exam – eat your heart out, Maths!

You are not expected to be perfect, fortunately – but you must try to reduce those careless slips...and the way to do it is to **proof-read**. Everyone knows that you should check your work, but for most students that means no more than a glance to see that it is still there! **Proof-reading** is a proper **word-by-word search** for corrections – just think how effective the search will be if you can find two, three, five, maybe ten small errors.

Task 5

Proof-read the following article and improve the accuracy of the spelling, punctuation and grammar.

A Problem for Teachers or Pupils?

Discipline, the meaning for discipline changes. For schools, mostly its one or two pupils shouting from the back of the class, asking all the teachers attention and changing the subject off the lesson. But I believe that it's not all these pupils fault.

From my experience my English lessons used to be the worst. I was put into the bottom set reserved for the not so bright and the pupils who would care about themselves and thought they were better than everyone. I was an A* pupil but only getting below C grades for English this was mainly due to the lack of teaching in my English class. The teacher didn't have a clue about teenagers or how to control the class. He thought by shouting and screaming, throttling things like a child having a tantrum, he would get his own way. He would keep the whole class behind even though it was only a select handful of pupils disrupting the lesson. After a few more lesson I started to forget the lesson and concentrate on other things such as my game console or a book I was reading. I had lost all respect for the teacher. While other teachers could walk into a class and be able to speak and joke with a class.

I believe the teachers must respect a pupil as much as a pupil must respect the teacher. The teacher must be able to react with the pupils, connect on a level with them to try and teach them but also to remember to make sure the pupils understand what is being said. But the argument isn't all blamed on the teachers. The small handful of pupils who shout, throw things or get like three year olds, can also be blamed.

There are other ways in which to control a class. If its 1 pupil disrupting ask them to go to another classroom or somewhere else such as a library or a senior member of a school to take the pupil to have 1 on 1 lessons.

If there isn't any were else the pupil can't go it makes the lesson much more difficult as it acts like a domino effect and when one starts another follows. A system needs to arrange in which it helps both pupils and teachers cope with discipline in the classroom, also if it gets to an extent maybe some way for another teacher to teach the class as so there can be some work done and the pupils who want to learn can have a chance at catching up with the system and not getting left behind.

Teachers all around the UK have to put up with a very small minority of students that go to school and disrupt the class. What can teachers do to help the students that want to learn and make a go at school and get something out of it at the end. This is the sort of things some teachers put up with just because the teacher tried to discipline the small minority as she is required. But what can the government and what can we do to help stop the small minority spoiling it for the students and for the teachers because how many people would stay in their job if they were threatened.

THE BRAINWASH BOX

- Sentences – don't let them run on and on.

- Punctuation – full stops are the thing.

- Spelling – think of patterns.

- Grammar – remember you're writing, not speaking.

- Proof-read your writing – hunt down your own errors.

Think – don't guess; write – don't scribble!

Unit 5.1 — Points and twists

RESPONDING TO EXTRACTS

'When I do extract questions, I don't bother to read the extract because it saves a bit of time and you can write more.'

The whole point of an extract question is to test your knowledge and understanding of a text in detail. You have to show that you can read closely and respond to a particular question by selecting relevant things to comment upon. You need to make points about the key moments when the drama twists and changes direction.

Two extracts, two questions

In the English Literature Specification A paper, you have to answer questions on two extracts, one from your set prose text and one from your set play.

This unit provides a drama extract for close study, plus questions that focus on the specific part of the play. You should be able to cope with the task even if you are not studying this particular play.

The text

Read the following extract from the play *An Inspector Calls* by J.B. Priestley. The play is about a young woman, Eva Smith, who committed suicide and several members of the Birling family, who employed her in their business and then sacked her. After her sacking, Eva Smith's fate is still linked to the Birlings. Sheila has had cause to complain about Eva's attitude as a sales assistant at Milwards fashion shop; Gerald, Sheila's fiancé, has had a relationship with Eva.

In this extract, the man investigating Eva Smith's death leaves Sheila and Gerald to talk about some of the revelations.

SHEILA: (*stormily*) Oh shut up, Eric. I know, I know. It's the only time I've done anything like that, and I'll never, never do it again to anybody. I've noticed them giving me a sort of look sometimes at Milwards – I noticed it even this afternoon – and I suppose some of them remember. I feel now I can never go there again. Oh – why had this to happen?

INSPECTOR: (*sternly*) That's what I asked myself tonight when I was looking at that dead girl. And then I said to myself: 'Well, we'll try to understand why it had to happen.' And that's why I'm here, and why I'm not going until I know all that happened. Eva Smith lost her job with Birling and company because the strike failed and they were determined not to have another one. At last she found another job – under what name I don't know – in a big shop, and had to leave there because you were annoyed with yourself and passed the annoyance on to her. Now she had to try something else. So first she changed her name to Daisy Renton –

GERALD: (*startled*) What?

INSPECTOR: (*steadily*) I said she changed her name to Daisy Renton.

GERALD: (*pulling himself together*) D'you mind if I give myself a drink, Sheila?
SHEILA merely nods, still staring at him, and he goes across to the tantalus on the sideboard for a whisky.

INSPECTOR: Where is your father, Miss Birling?

SHEILA: He went into the drawing-room to tell my mother what was happening here. Eric, take the Inspector along to the drawing-room.
As ERIC moves, the INSPECTOR looks from SHEILA to GERALD, then goes out with ERIC.
Well, Gerald?

GERALD: (*trying to smile*) Well what, Sheila?

SHEILA: How did you come to know this girl – Eva Smith?

GERALD: I didn't.

SHEILA: Daisy Renton then – it's the same thing.

GERALD: Why should I have known her?

SHEILA: Oh don't be stupid. We haven't much time. You gave yourself away as soon as he mentioned her other name.

GERALD: All right. I knew her. Let's leave it at that.

SHEILA: We can't leave it at that.

GERALD: (*approaching her*) Now listen darling –

SHEILA: No, that's no use. You not only knew her but you knew her very well. Otherwise, you wouldn't look so guilty about it. When did you first get to know her?

He does not reply.

Was it after she left Milwards? When she changed her name, as he said, and began to lead a different sort of life? Were you seeing her last spring and summer, during that time when you hardly came near me and said you were so busy? Were you?

He does not reply but looks at her.

Yes, of course you were.

GERALD: I'm sorry, Sheila. But it was all over and done with last summer. I hadn't set eyes on the girl for at least six months. I don't come into this suicide business.

SHEILA: I thought I didn't, half an hour ago.

GERALD: You don't. Neither of us does. So – for God's sake – don't say anything to the Inspector.

SHEILA: About you and this girl?

GERALD: Yes. We can keep it from him.

SHEILA: (*laughs rather hysterically*) Why – you fool – *he knows*. Of course he knows. And I hate to think how much he knows that we don't know yet. You'll see. You'll see.

She looks at him almost in triumph. He looks crushed. The door slowly opens and the INSPECTOR *appears, looking steadily and searchingly at them.*

INSPECTOR: Well?

The question

Now consider the following two-part question:

- **(i) What do you think of the way Sheila speaks and behaves here?**
  (ii) How do you think an audience would respond to this part of the play?

Before you write your response, look closely at the sample answer and the comments and boxes that follow it.

SAMPLE ANSWER

(i) In this scene of the play Sheila is the main spokesperson. She doesn't say as much as some of the other people but what she says is very strong in feeling.

The way in which Sheila speaks and behaves at the beginning of the scene makes us feel that Sheila is very sorry for her behaviour in the shop earlier in the play. She is also sorry about the outcome of her behaviour.

'It's the only time I've ever done anything like that, and I'll never, never do anything like that to anybody again.'

This shows that Sheila is not a terrible person and didn't mean to bring harm to anyone.

Further on is the scene Sheila and Gerald are left on their own in the room. This builds up the tension, and by leaving two young lovers alone in the room makes us focus on them, especially Sheila. Sheila's behaviour changes again and she speaks to Gerald in a different tone. She is trying to get to the bottom of the incident and how Gerald knows Eva Smith. She speaks to him in quite a nasty way. Also in this scene Sheila's behaviour towards Gerald changes.

Sheila questions him about Eva Smith, and the way she does this suggests that she had some suspicions before this event.

(ii) I think an audience would feel some sympathy for Sheila in this part of the play. I think this because she accepts her guilt in the death of Eva Smith, but didn't mean any harm. Also they would be surprised that Gerald had an affair because he is a very nice man throughout the play.

The audience's response to Gerald probably wouldn't be a very good one because he has been having an affair. Also he is trying to pretend he didn't have anything to do with her and her death.

COMMENT

The student makes a few relevant points but the whole answer could be much improved. It is very generalized and the quotation could be more streamlined – shorter quote, sharper comment. The drama and tension of the moment are not well brought out in the answer. The stage directions and the impact of the shock revelations are not well represented. Sheila's words are not well tracked. In the second part of the answer, the audience's likely reactions need also to be pinpointed at key moments. There will possibly be mixed reactions, so a simple 'one-dimensional' right-wrong view is not likely to be very convincing.

You can do better

In your own response, try to convey the drama and tension of the moment by being more precise and engaged about the text.

Take note of Sheila's reactions: from '*stormily*' to '*laughs rather hysterically*'.

Comment on the climax of the scene where '*She looks at him almost in triumph. He looks crushed...*' as the Inspector returns to the room.

Your answer may be in two parts or it could be just one piece of continuous response. Either approach is acceptable – provided both the character's performance and the audience's reactions are given due attention.

THE BRAINWASH BOX

- Stick to the extract.
- Answer the question.
- If it's a play, think about the drama!

Change the question!

- (i) **What do you think of the Inspector here?**
  (ii) **What do you think of the way Sheila and Gerald respond to him?**

CHECKLIST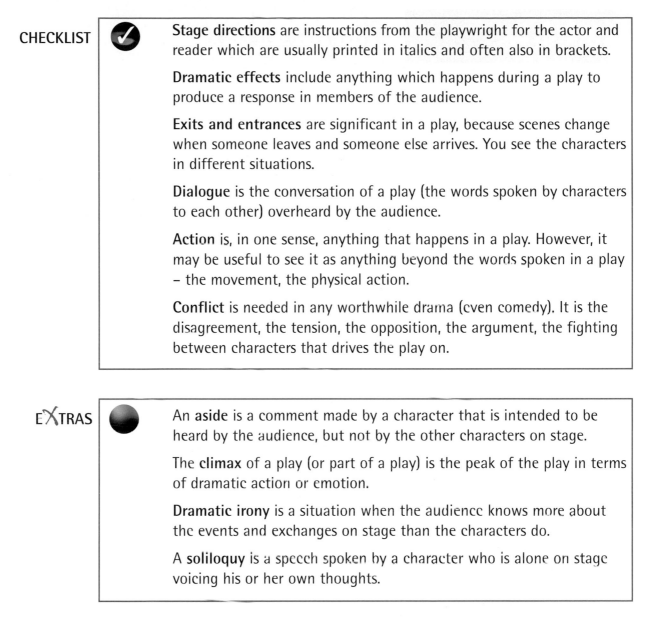

Stage directions are instructions from the playwright for the actor and reader which are usually printed in italics and often also in brackets.

Dramatic effects include anything which happens during a play to produce a response in members of the audience.

Exits and entrances are significant in a play, because scenes change when someone leaves and someone else arrives. You see the characters in different situations.

Dialogue is the conversation of a play (the words spoken by characters to each other) overheard by the audience.

Action is, in one sense, anything that happens in a play. However, it may be useful to see it as anything beyond the words spoken in a play – the movement, the physical action.

Conflict is needed in any worthwhile drama (even comedy). It is the disagreement, the tension, the opposition, the argument, the fighting between characters that drives the play on.

EXTRAS

An aside is a comment made by a character that is intended to be heard by the audience, but not by the other characters on stage.

The climax of a play (or part of a play) is the peak of the play in terms of dramatic action or emotion.

Dramatic irony is a situation when the audience knows more about the events and exchanges on stage than the characters do.

A soliloquy is a speech spoken by a character who is alone on stage voicing his or her own thoughts.

Focus on the extract by annotating it.

Unit 5.2

shaping ideas

DISCURSIVE ESSAY QUESTIONS

'I'll write out bits of the story – that'll take up a bit of space.'

Essays on set texts in a closed-book exam (i.e. you can't have the books with you) can make you very nervous. Will you be able to answer any of the questions? Will you remember anything about the books? Will you be able to think of any quotations? In other words, will your mind 'go blank'?

Think positive

If you are reasonably well prepared, you should not have any shocks in the exam.

1. The questions are fair. They are designed to find out what you know, not what you don't know. They are not intended to trip you up.
2. Many of the questions have the support of bullet points that give prompts to help you through your essay.
3. Thoughtful personal response is encouraged – you are not looking for a single right answer.

'Learning' essays and hoping they fit the questions asked in the exams is bad practice – don't do it!

The question

Consider this essay question on *Of Mice and Men*:

- **What do you think of Curley?**

Think about:
- his first appearance, in Chapter 2
- his relationships with the other characters
- the fight with Lennie
- the end of the story
- the way he speaks and behaves.

Practise your technique

Of Mice and Men by John Steinbeck is one of the most popular set texts. You may actually be studying it. If you are, you should try the Curley question yourself OR structure a question (with bullet-points) on one of the other characters.

If you are not studying this book, you can still look closely at the sample response and the comment on the way the essay is written. You can construct a question on either your set novel or your set play.

Before you start, look at the sample answer.

This essay is written by someone early in their GCSE course. It is their first-ever attempt at a timed essay in 40 minutes.

Read it and, as you do so, think of constructive suggestions that you could make.

SAMPLE ANSWER

When Curley first appeared in the story, I thought to myself, 'what an idiot he is' and by the time I had finished reading the story, I still thought the same! Curley is someone who likes to take advantage of someone else when he sees a weakness in them. He is just like a bully, who doesn't care about anyone else bar himself. The only person that he has respect for is Slim. This could be because he is scared of Slim, or he has had a fight with him in the past and did not succeed. Curley also treats everyone like a piece of mud, and speaks to them rudely all the time. If he wants respect off people, then he just can't go shouting at his workers for no reason. He can also be very aggressive at times which is not going to please people and earn him respect.

When Curley first enters the story, he walks into the bunks looking for his father, but as he turns round to leave, he spots George and Lennie. Immediately after he sees them, he bends his elbow and tenses his fists. This tells me that he likes to pick fights because he thinks he's strong and tough and he may think that by doing this it will make George and Lennie scared and respect him, but some cases like this one, this does not work. Curley then begins to question the boys, but soon gets annoyed and frustrated when George answers for Lennie. This tells me that Curley thinks that he is more important than everyone else and is better than everyone else, so if I was George, I would be starting to not like this guy already, and I wouldn't give him any respect. Also, if he speaks like this to anyone else, I wouldn't think that they would like him either.

Looking back at the story, I would say that Curley is quite lonely. I think this because he treats everyone with disrespect so I don't think many people are going to like him, so he is mainly on his own. He is also disliked by his wife because he treats her badly, so he is pretty much on his own most of the time. This could lead to depressions, but it is his own fault. Although he treats his wife badly, I'd say he loves her very much, because he gets very paranoid when his wife talks to other people and when he finds out that his wife had been killed he becomes very distraught and immediately goes to kill Lennie for what he has done.

Before Lennie kills Curley's wife, Lennie and Curley have a fight. Curley begins to pick on Lennie in the bunks for no reason, and begins to punch Lennie repeatedly. Curley may be trying to send a message to everyone saying that Curley should not be messed with, but this plan backfires when Lennie decides to stick up for himself, and starts to fight back.

COMMENT

This is an excellent first effort. It is likely that the student learned a lot just by taking stock of the experience.

1. He has tried to answer the question from the very start. 'Idiot' though is not the best word to summarize Curley. He may be foolish to behave in the way he does, but some stronger words of criticism are needed to describe him. He is not a nice man!

2. After the introductory paragraph, the student has tried to follow the bullet-points, but has misjudged the time. The effect is an unbalanced essay that deals less well with each of the later bullet-points. He needs to be more sharply aware of what he wants to write in each paragraph. He seems set on writing advice for Curley to improve his image!

3. For an extra trick, the student needs to filter in the words and phrases that will show an awareness of the time and place of the book. There is no real sense of the ranch, the isolation, the 'man's world', the American cowboy. Think of John Steinbeck and what he might have been trying to tell us.

In summary, a better balance, a sharper style and a greater awareness of the writer are all needed to make this a C grade essay. It seems a lot, but it isn't!

THE BRAINWASH BOX

- Answer directly.
- Use the supporting bullet-points.
- Organize in paragraphs.
- Use details from the text.

Change the question!

- **Which character do you have most sympathy for? Write about your chosen character, explaining why you feel sympathy for him/her.**

CHECKLIST

An **essay** is a continuous piece of writing on a subject. In English Literature, you would not expect to see sub-headings or sections or illustrations in an essay – therefore the use of **paragraphs** is an essential part of the structure.

Discursive writing in English Literature requires you to organize your own selection of facts and opinions to respond to a fairly open task or question. In fact, a discursive essay is a **one-way discussion**, so you have to work hard to keep to the question.

EXTRAS

In a closed-book exam, you show your knowledge and understanding of your set novel and set play by **direct quotation** or other types of **evidence**.

Direct reference and **detailed knowledge** can be shown through confident use of names, specific details, paraphrase AND very short, integrated quotations (**usually a word or a phrase**).

You have time to think before you start to write.

Unit 5.3

Getting inside a character

EMPATHY QUESTIONS

'There's a choice of questions anyway, so you don't have to do an empathy question.'

In an empathy task, you have to pretend to be a character from a text. An empathy question is often set as an alternative to an essay question. Both types of question test your understanding, so an empathy task should not be seen as something out of bounds. You should have an open mind about any empathy question that is on offer and judge it properly against the other option. If you just disregard it, you may be throwing away a great opportunity to write convincingly.

Get inside the character

In an empathy task, you write down directly the character's imaginary words. You need to show that:

- you can select key parts of the story
- you know what the character thinks and feels
- you know how the character speaks.

The question

Consider this essay question on *Blood Brothers*:

- **Imagine you are Mrs Lyons. At the end of the play you think back over what has happened. Write your thoughts and feelings. Remember how Mrs Lyons would speak when you write your answer.**

Think about:
- your feelings about Mrs Johnstone
- your relationship with Edward
- your feelings about all that has happened.

Practise your technique

Blood Brothers by Willy Russell is a modern play on the set text list for English Literature. If you are studying the play, you can either write your own response to this task before you read on or after you have looked at the sample answer.

If you are not studying *Blood Brothers*, you can still look closely at the sample response and comment on the way it is written. Then choose a character from one of your own set texts and write the thoughts and feelings of your character in a convincing way.

Remember that there may be empathy tasks set for either your prose or your drama text.

Blood Brothers is the story of twin brothers who are separated at birth. Micky stays with the natural mother, Mrs Johnstone, while the childless Mrs Lyons persuades Mrs Johnstone to part with Eddie.

Their lives become intertwined, but only at the end of the play does Micky find out about Eddie. Micky resents that he too was not given to a wealthy family. He shoots Eddie and then is shot by the police. Mrs Lyons' speech needs to reflect a great depth of feeling.

SAMPLE ANSWER

It's all her fault. Why couldn't she leave us alone? Why? I and Edward were getting along really well, like butterflies in a field, especially when we moved. No. No, she had to follow us. She, she had to move didn't she. Like they say a leech is attracted to blood, she is the same. A leech. Always interfering with his life. I mean she has really done it now. She has killed her son, and also mine. First it was the locket. Why on earth did she give him that? Not as if he had good times down there, in that filthy place. Always getting my Edward into trouble.

I should've stabbed her when I had the chance, then none of this would've ended in a disaster. What am I going to do with myself now. Now that my heart has been ripped out by that witch and used to wipe the floor with. Blast you woman!

Oh my Edward! You had everything for yourself. A good house to live in, parents that loved and adored you, a fantastic education and people respected you. Your job was perfect and so was your life. Why oh why did you go back. Why did you get involved with Mickey and his wife Linda. You didn't need her. You could have had any woman you wanted, why her?

I remember when we moved, and how much you enjoyed playing in the garden with your father, and enjoying freedom and happiness. Yes happiness. How proud I was of you, leading your school to cricket success. Like your father cricket mad. But your education, now you were the brightest and well dressed. Tears of happiness in my eyes when you came back home from your first term in school. We were so proud of you Edward. And we still are.

Throughout the course of my life I have been with you, I thought nothing could separate us, not even death. But look at her now. Pretending to feel sorry for herself. I swear I'll kill her! If she never wanted anything like this to happen, she would of left us all alone and let us get on with our lives. It's not as if we never took care of Edward. I did. More than what she can look back at her children. Edward was a business man, kind, generous, respected. Not a lot like her Mickey! He could not even support his family. For god's sake, he had No Job.

Edward come back, prove them all wrong. SHE has taken everything away from me. Wait Mrs. Johnstone, Wait! I will ruin you the same way you have ruined me, my husbands life. And YOU have ended Edwards life for good.

COMMENT

This is a passionate, engaged response. It is a convincing interpretation of the character, with excellent textual reference.

It is a very clear C grade and it begins to match the requirements for a higher grade because of the quite convincing representation of the character.

THE BRAINWASH BOX

- Speak directly as the character.
- Think like the character.
- Get the character's feelings.
- Remember you are looking back from the end of the story.

Change the question!

- **Imagine you are giving advice to someone who is going to take the part of _____. Tell him or her how he or she should present the character to an audience. If you wish, you may focus on specific parts of the play.**

Think about:
- the way you think _____ should speak and behave with other characters
- the way you think he or she should show his or her thoughts and feelings.

CHECKLIST ✓

A **director** supervises and instructs actors who are appearing in the production of a play.

Empathy is the ability to understand and share the feelings of others.

Sympathy is the feeling of pity and sorrow for someone else's misfortune.

A **monologue** is a long speech by one actor (character) in a play.

EXTRAS ●

A **theme** is an important idea or subject that runs through a text.

Some of the themes evident in *Blood Brothers* are: **childhood and adolescence; social class; surrogate parenthood** and **superstition**.

However, it is not enough to spot that a theme runs through a text. You need to be able to explain how the characters and plot contribute to the theme, and what the writer is trying to say about the theme.

Empathy responses need the direct voice of the character.

Unit 5.4

Into the unknown

'UNSEEN' POETRY APPRECIATION

' How can you write about it if it's invisible?! ...'

The final section of the English Literature Specification A exam requires you to write about a poem. It will be a poem that you have not studied specifically in preparation for the exam. It is called an 'unseen' poem, because the chances are that you will not have seen it before. You are expected to 'read and respond' thoughtfully, using your reading skills to show some understanding and appreciation of the poem.

You should read as many poems as you can during your GCSE course, because confidence is everything! Have you only read three or four poems? Have you relied on your teacher to give you every last crumb of information about them? If so, you will not be able to function successfully in the exam.

Poetry is obviously different in some ways from prose and drama, but don't make too much of the fact. Concentrate on the words and sentences as they occur in sequence, just as you would with a prose extract.

Remember the poet chooses the words and the word order very carefully. The poem on the exam paper will be short, so every word will count. Every word will contribute to the meaning of the poem.

The text

Read the poem 'Tramp' by William Marshall.

Tramp

He liked he said
rainbows in the sky
and children
who passed him in the
street
without staring.
And he liked he said the
ordinary things
like
roses in snow
and the way he
remembered
the first time
the first time he
really smelt the
rain on
a green hillside
back home
just before the sun died.
And he liked he said
thinking about
who slept beneath the red
brick roofs he
walked by in the
early part of the day
from Land's End to John O'Groats.
But he said
as a full time tramp with no
other place to go he
was worried
where he would die –
Land's End or John O'Groats.

William Marshall

The question

Now consider the following question:

- **Write about the poem and its effect on you.**

You may wish to include some or all of these points:

- the poem's content – what it is about
- the ideas the poet may have wanted us to think about
- the mood or atmosphere of the poem
- how it is written – words or phrases you find interesting, the way the poem is structured or organized, and so on
- your response to the poem.

CHECKLIST ✓ **Annotation** means adding short notes and explanations to a text, in this case a poem. You can write on your exam paper to sort out your thoughts on the poem.

Voice and **situation** are key starting points for understanding a poem. You do not need to be exact, but you need to avoid mis-readings. The voice is not the tramp, but a spokesperson for the tramp who is reporting the tramp's views. The situation described is not precise, but it seems to be a selection of the tramp's memories and opinions, leading to the final, sad thought about death.

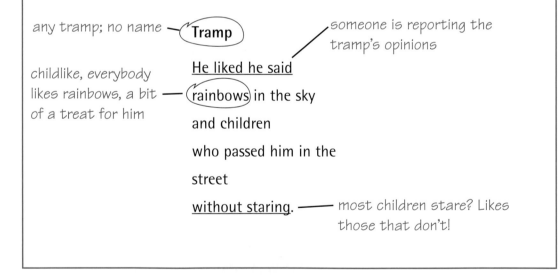

Try to write your response this time BEFORE you read the sample answer.

Note: Land's End (Cornwall) and John O'Groats (North of Scotland) are at the extreme opposite points of the mainland of Great Britain.

SAMPLE ANSWER

The poem 'Tramp' is about a tramp who describes what he enjoys seeing in the world, and what he doesn't. This tramp says that he likes, 'rainbows in the sky and children who passed him in the street without staring'. This also tells me that he may not like to be stared at and people feeling sorry for him, or judging him on the way he looks.

The tramp also says that he likes ordinary things like roses in snow, and he also likes to remember old times, and the way he first smelt rain on a green hillside. He also likes to think of the people who live under red bricked roofs, as he walked past them. The tramp thinks this every morning, when on his daily walk (or so I would expect reading the passage), from Lands End to John O'Groats. He then goes on to talk about where he will die. He is worried, because he doesn't know where he is going to die, Lands End, or John O'Groats? He worries about this because he is a full time tramp, and has no other place to go.

I think the poet wanted us to think about how awful and frightening living as a tramp is. I think that he is trying to make us think that being a tramp is the last straw in life, we should always keep trying to get jobs, and earn enough for a living. He is also trying to tell us that there are lots of questions to be asked if you're a tramp, a lot of 'what ifs' and 'where am I going to die?' However, although I have said this, I also think that the poet is saying enjoy life while you can, and never take it for granted.

I would say that this poem is more of a sad one than a happy one. I think the mood of this poem is sad, but in a happy way. It is saying about the tramp and where he will die which is very sad, someone who could die any time and don't know where they will die, but the things he likes, and describes are happy. It is a bit like he is saying thank you for his life.

This poem is written in a nice style. I like this because it makes me feel that there are always 'key' words after most long lines in the poem, like 'He liked he said

> Rainbows in the sky
> And children
> Who passed him in the
> Street
> Without staring.'

I think that 'street' and 'without staring' are the key words in this sentence because the tramp may only ever stay on and around streets, and he also may not like people who stare at him, thinking things about him, especially children. I feel like the rest of the poem is written like this, so I very much do like this style of writing.

On the whole, I would say that I enjoyed reading 'Tramp' by William Marshall and would most certainly recommend it to others and definitely read it again. I found it very interesting and for me, it was a little insight to the life of a full time tramp.

COMMENT

This is another fine effort from a student at the start of a GCSE course. The response shows that the student has the confidence to say what he feels. However, the answer could have been shorter because there are some loose and rather vague parts.

Points to consider:
*   The student understands clearly that there are good and bad features of a tramp's existence, but that it is not a lifestyle that we really envy.
*   He wasn't told that Land's End and John O'Groats are about 900 miles from each other, so we can't blame him for thinking the tramp walked the distance every day! However, the real issue about walking and, eventually, dying 'on the road' is solitude, mixed with uncertainty and fear.
*   The student lacks a bit of confidence in using quotations, though he certainly showed promising signs of wanting to pick out details to comment on.
*   Comments on style (the words) and structure (the shape) are difficult. You could say the style is simple (with random bits of detail) and the structure is long and loose (wandering along aimlessly?), but see such comments as a bonus rather than an essential requirement.

All in all, this student has written a borderline C grade response.

THE BRAINWASH BOX
*   Read the poem carefully, more than once.
*   Annotate the poem quickly.
*   Cover the bullet-point prompts OR cover the stages of the poem.
*   Comment on key details.

Change the question?

No!

Change the poem!

The instructions remain the same every year for the 'unseen' poetry question. Sometimes there is a sentence of explanation to set you off in the right direction in your response.

In the following poem, the poet Gillian Clarke describes the power of a peregrine falcon.

- **Write about the poem and its effect on you**.

You may wish to include some or all of these points:
- the poem's content – what it is about
- the ideas the poet may have wanted us to think about
- the mood or atmosphere of the poem
- how it is written – words or phrases you find interesting, the way the poem is structured or organized, and so on
- your response to the poem.

Peregrine Falcon

New blood in the killing-ground,
her scullery,
her boneyard.

I touch the raw wire
of vertigo
feet from the edge.

Her house is air. She comes downstairs
on a turn of wind.
This is her table.

She is arrow.
At two miles a minute
the pigeon bursts like a city.

While we turned our backs
she wasted nothing
but a rose-ringed foot

still warm.

Gillian Clarke

E**X**TRAS

> An **image** in poetry (or writing generally) is a **picture** created in the mind of the reader by words in the poem.
>
> On a simple **descriptive** level, **literal** images can be effective, e.g. 'children who passed him in the street', 'roses in snow' (both taken from 'Tramp'). The reader sees those things in an uncomplicated way.
>
> **Similes** and **metaphors** are non-literal or **figurative** images. They are often used to put more challenging images in your mind. They are images built upon **comparisons** and these are often unusual and thought-provoking. A **simile** is an **indirect comparison** using *like* or *as* to link one thing to the other. A **metaphor** is a **direct comparison**, often using *is* to make the clearest possible association.
>
> Examples:
>
> *'The pigeon bursts like a city'* (**simile**) is shocking and stops you in your tracks;
>
> *'She is arrow'* (**metaphor**) portrays the speed, accuracy and deadliness of the falcon in a phrase of three words.
>
> *'This is her table'* (**metaphor/personification**) makes an unlikely comparison with domestic human dining.
>
> *'The sun died'* (**metaphor/personification**) is suggestive, putting in mind the end of the day and perhaps something stronger too.
>
> It really does not matter if you cannot distinguish between the different types of images or if you cannot remember any of the technical terms. What matters is that you can respond to the words of the poem in a thoughtful, sensitive way.

Apply your usual reading skills to the poem – don't panic because it's a poem.

ANTHOLOGY COMPARISON TASKS

´You mean we get a fresh copy of the anthology to look at in the exam? That'll help my revision – it means I won't have to do any!´

English Literature candidates who are entering Specification B study the WJEC Anthology. This contains <u>eight</u> short stories and a group of poems by each of <u>three</u> poets. A large part of the exam focuses on the details of these short stories and poems. Some of the anthology questions on prose and poetry involve **comparison** skills.

Organization is the key

When you are answering a comparison question, you need to be clearly organized. It needs to be clear at all times which of the texts you are referring to. You should be confident enough to make any point of comparison that occurs to you when you are writing – BUT – the easiest way to organizing your essay clearly is to write first about one text, then the other. Simple, but successful.

The questions are geared to you using your fresh copy of the Anthology during the exam – because the focus is on textual detail – but you can't expect to do your best if you don't revise the full range of stories and poems.

CHECKLIST ✔

An **anthology** is a collection of writing by different authors published together in one book.

When you make a **comparison**, you say that one thing is like another in some way. A **contrast** is a clear difference between two texts.

Similarities are features that might bring two texts into close comparison. However, they are **not identical**.

Differences are features that set two texts apart. However, they are **not opposites**.

In comparison work, you can **cross-reference**, which means that you can refer to a point of comparison with another text.

> However, you can explore effective **connections** between texts by writing about one text alone and then making **parallel comments** about a second text. It is important that the whole response has a **balance** between the first half and the second half.

The texts

Read the opening paragraphs of two short stories that feature in the sample answer to the question discussed in this unit. The two stories were chosen by the candidate from the choice of eight short stories available in the WJEC Anthology.

The story openings are from 'Extraordinary Little Cough' by Dylan Thomas and 'The Lesson' by Toni Cade Bambara.

The opening to:

'Extraordinary Little Cough' by Dylan Thomas

One afternoon, in a particularly bright and glowing August, some years before I knew I was happy, George Hooping, whom we called Little Cough, Sidney Evans, Dan Davies, and I sat on the roof of a lorry travelling to the end of the Peninsula. It was a tall, six-wheeled lorry, from which we could spit on the roofs of the passing cars and throw our apple stumps at women on the pavement. One stump caught a man on a bicycle in the middle of the back, he swerved across the road, for a moment we sat quiet and George Hooping's face grew pale. And if the lorry runs him over, I thought calmly as the man on the bicycle swayed towards the hedge, he'll get killed and I'll be sick on my trousers and perhaps on Sidney's too, and we'll be arrested and hanged, except George Hooping who didn't have an apple.

But the lorry swept past; behind us, the bicycle drove into the hedge, the man stood up and waved his fist, and I waved my cap back at him.

'You shouldn't have waved your cap,' said Sidney Evans, 'he'll know what school we're in.' He was clever, dark, and careful, and had a purse and a wallet.

'We're not in school now.'

'Nobody can expel me,' said Dan Davies. He was leaving next term to serve in his father's fruit shop for a salary.

We all wore haversacks, except George Hooping whose mother had given him a brown-paper parcel that kept coming undone, and carried a suitcase each. I had placed a coat over my suitcase because the initials on it were 'N.T.' and everybody would know that it belonged to my sister. Inside the lorry were two tents, a box of food, a packing-case of kettles and saucepans and knives and forks, an oil lamp, a primus stove, ground sheets and blankets, a gramophone with three records, and a tablecloth from George Hooping's mother.

We were going to camp for a fortnight in Rhossilli, in a field above the sweeping five-mile beach. Sidney and Dan had stayed there last year, coming back brown and swearing, full of stories of campers' dances round the fires at midnight, and elderly girls from the training college who sun-bathed naked on ledges of rocks surrounded by laughing boys, and singing in bed that lasted until dawn. But George had never left home for more than a night; and then, he told me, one half-holiday when it was raining and there was nothing to do but stay in the washhouse racing his guineapigs giddily along the benches, it was only to stay in St Thomas, three miles from his house, with an aunt who could see through the walls and who knew what a Mrs Hoskin was doing in the kitchen.

The opening to:
'The Lesson' by Toni Cade Bambara

Back in the days when everyone was old and stupid or young and foolish and me and Sugar were the only ones just right, this lady moved on our block with nappy hair and proper speech and no makeup. And quite naturally we laughed at her, laughed the way we did at the junk man who went about his business like he was some big-time president and his sorry-ass horse his secretary. And we kinda hated her too, hated the way we did the winos who cluttered up our parks and pissed on our handball walls and stank up our hallways and stairs so you couldn't halfway play hide-and-seek without a goddamn gas mask. Miss Moore was her name. The only woman on the block with no first name. And she was always planning these boring-ass things for us to do, us being my cousin, mostly, who lived on the block cause we all moved North the same time and to the same apartment then spread out gradual to breathe. And our parents would yank our heads into some kinda shape and crisp up our clothes so we'd be presentable for travel with Miss Moore, who always looked like she was going to church, though she never did. Which is just one of things the grown-ups talked about when they talked behind her back like a dog. But when she came calling with some sachet she'd sewed up or some gingerbread she'd made or some book, why then they'd all be too embarrassed to turn her down and we'd get handed over all spruced up. She'd been to college and said it was only right that she should take responsibility for the young ones' education, and she not even related by marriage or blood. So they'd go for it. Specially Aunt Gretchen. She was the main gofer in the family. You got some ole dumb shit foolishness you want somebody to go for, you send Aunt Gretchen. She been screwed into the go-along for so long, it's a blood-deep natural thing with her. Which is how she got saddled with me and Sugar and Junior in the first place while our mothers were in a la-de-da apartment up the block having a good ole time.

The question

Now consider the following question:

- **Choose two stories you think open well. Look at about the first 30 lines of each. Show how each opening is interesting for the reader.**

In your answer write about:
- what happens in the opening
- what we learn about the characters
- the setting of the story
- anything else you find interesting.

SAMPLE ANSWER

Two stories that I believe open well are 'Extraordinary Little Cough' by Dylan Thomas and 'The Lesson' by Toni Cade Bambara.

The first thing that I notice about the beginning of 'Extraordinary Little Cough' is how quickly it introduces us to the main characters of the story. I feel that this makes the story easier to understand. The four boys George Hooping aka Little Cough, Sidney Evans, Dan Davies and the narrator are on the roof of a Lorry heading to the end of the Peninsula. Now we have all of the characters, a location and a heading, eg what they are doing/going. All of this in the first five lines. I think that this is a good characteristic of the story.

We also learn a lot about the characters early on. The way the boys act shows us that they are quite careless and maybe even yobbish. 'Spit on the roofs at passing cars and throw our apple stumps at women.'

We also get the impression the narrator is quite childish; when they hit a man on a bicycle with an apple stump he is worried that they might be arrested and hanged and also that he would be sick on his trousers. We learn that Sidney Evans is more clever and cunning.

'You shouldn't have waved your cap', said Sidney Evans, 'he'll know what school we're in.'

We learn more of George Hooping, he soon appears different to the boys in the fact that he doesn't have a haversack, he seems almost isolated from the group. Lines 25 to 30 tell us exactly where the boys are heading; this sets the stage for the rest of the story.

'The Lesson' is set in a deprived suburb of an American city. We learn this both through the text and by the way the characters act and talk. We learn of the characters Sugar, the writer, Miss Moore early on in the story. Sugar and the writer come across as crude and uncaring at first because they laugh at Miss Moore who is obviously different. Miss Moore is isolated because she was 'The only woman on the block with no first name.'

This shows us that she intended to be different. We soon learn that Miss Moore is a well educated woman, she is a responsible and moral person who is concerned for the children's welfare.

The parents of the children come across as being shallow and two faced. They talk about Miss Moore behind her back.

COMMENT

This response has a succession of tightly written, good quality points about each of the openings. There is a clear focus on the openings and the bullet-points; there are nicely matched comments on each story; there is strongly implied understanding of the whole stories. The ability to place the understanding of the two texts side by side so comfortably suggests a clear C grade – so it may be a little bit harsh to note that there is rather more commentary on the first story opening than the second.

THE BRAINWASH BOX

- Back your own thoughts about the stories and poems.
- Cover the two selected texts equally.
- Don't complicate by criss-crossing the texts frequently.

Change the question!

- **Some of the poems in the Anthology deal with memories. Choose two poems by different poets. Examine the ways in which the poets write about memories.**

In your answer write about:
- what the poet is remembering
- how each poet describes the memory
- how you react to each poem
- words and phrases you find interesting.

EXTRAS

The Anthology contains stories and poems. These are short texts compared with full-length plays and novels. However, even though they are short, poems and stories too have an opening, a middle and an ending.

At the beginning, they pose **questions** and they create **expectations**; later, they have **development** in **stages**; finally, they have **outcomes** and **conclusions**.

The reader's **overview** is a **general understanding** of the **whole** text. The last section may be critical to an understanding – the final paragraph or two of a story, the final sentence or two of a poem. Don't ignore the ending of a short story or a poem.

Divide your time equally between the two texts.

Unit 6.1

Focus on ENGLISH PAPER 1

' You can't revise for English, can you? It's just how it goes on the day, isn't it?'

You can and MUST revise for GCSE English. Use specimen (and past) papers and practise your skills 'against the clock'.

Do not leave anything to chance!

To get the most from the next few pages, you should have a copy of a WJEC Paper 1 examination in front of you.

Note: The number of marks and questions in Paper 1 changed slightly in 2004. For this exercise, do not refer to a Paper 1 from earlier than 2004.

Answers to the questions raised in the 'Know the Exam' boxes are in the *Teacher's Guide*.

The front page

The paper lasts **two hours**. The best candidates use the full time. If you are aiming for your best possible result, you too must work for the full two hours.

KNOW THE EXAM

1. Check the front page to see how many minutes you are advised to spend on each part of the paper.

   Section A?   Section B   Question B1?   Question B2?

   How many marks for Section A? How many for Section B?

SECTION A: READING (FICTION)

This section tests your understanding of a narrative (short story).

First, you should read the whole story and then look through the questions.

Most questions will be worth 10 marks; some questions may be worth 5 marks.

KNOW THE EXAM

> 2. a) How long do you think your 10 mark answers should be?
>
>   b) How much time should you spend on a 10 mark answer?

The line numbers

In Section A of Paper 1, the lines of the story will be numbered. For most questions, you will be directed to particular lines of the story: (**Look again at lines**...). You must use material just from those lines for your answer.

KNOW THE EXAM

> 3. Can you think of an idea that will help you to stick to the correct lines when answering a question?

The section will probably end with a question based on the whole story. Look out for these words, or something like them:

- **To answer the next question you will need to consider the passage as a whole.**

When you answer a question on the whole story, try to deal with the beginning, the middle and the end of the story. That means that you must judge which bits to pick out and how much to write about them.

Focus on questions

Now look at a typical set of questions for Section A on Paper 1. The first question, worth 5 marks, tells you to '**List**...', so make sure that you do. It is a 'location' question, otherwise known as 'search-and-find'. You need to do no more than pick out five details and write them in a list.

Look out for these words, or something like them:

- **Look again at lines...**
  List five details from these lines that...   **(5)**

KNOW THE EXAM

4. What is the best way of answering a question with the instruction 'List...'?

The next question is worth 10 marks, so it requires a longer answer than the previous one. It contains the key phrase '**your thoughts and feelings**' that means your personal response is needed. The words '**refer to the text**' should remind you to back up your personal response with evidence. The bullet-points supporting the question should help you to organize your answer. Look out for these words, or something like them:

- **Look again at lines...**
  What are your thoughts and feelings about...? You must refer to the text to support the points you make.

  You should consider:
  o   **what happens**
  o   **what he says and does**
  o   **how he is described.**   **(10)**

KNOW THE EXAM

5. a) What words at the start of your sentences will help you give a personal response?

   b) What different ways can you think of to 'refer to the text'?

   c) How will the bullet-points in the question help you to organize your answer?

The next question is worth 5 marks, but it is more than just search-and-find. You can get some marks by simply lifting from the text, but you must try to use your own words where possible. Look out for these words, or something like them:

- **Look again at lines...**
  How does ...... react when ......?   **(5)**

KNOW THE EXAM

6. When you successfully use your own words in an answer, what does it show the examiner?

Now we are on to another question worth 10 marks. You need to do more than write one or two sentences, else you will only score one or two marks! Look out for these words, or something like them:

- **Look again at lines…**
  What are your impressions of … …? How does the writer create these impressions? (10)

Impressions, in this sense, are thoughts and feelings, ideas and opinions. You should feel reasonably free to write down your personal views.

Do not forget the 'how' part of the question. Try to find relevant words and phrases from the text to back up your points. Your answer will be marked as a single response, not in two parts, but you must not ignore the second question.

KNOW THE EXAM

7. Do you think it is easier to treat the two questions above as separate tasks or to link the relevant words and phrases with the points being made?

The empathy question

Finally in this section, an entirely different kind of question – an empathy task. Look out for these words, or something like them:

- **To answer this question you must consider the passage as a whole. Imagine you are … … You tell your best friend your thoughts and feelings about what has happened. Write what you say.** (10)

In an empathy task, remember that you have to pretend to be the character named in the question. You have to speak about what has happened from the character's point of view. (Note that Section A does not always have an empathy question.)

KNOW THE EXAM

8. Apart from saying what has happened in parts of the story, what do you need to do to write a good 'empathy' response?

THE BRAINWASH BOX

- Do not miss out any questions.

- Answer them in the correct order.

- Ten-mark answers should all be half a page long (on average); five-mark answers should be shorter.

SECTION B: DESCRIPTIVE AND IMAGINATIVE WRITING

In this section, your writing skills will be tested. You have to do two pieces of writing. Watch your spelling, punctuation, sentence structure and grammar at all times. Remember to use paragraphs.

Look at the front page of your examination paper. Remind yourself how much time you should spend on Questions B1 and B2.

Now, turn to page 4 of your examination paper.

Describe the...

B1 is the descriptive writing task. You have no choice in this question. Expect a task that will instruct you to write about a place.

B1. Describe the scene...

You should write about a page in your answer book.

Remember that this is a test of your ability to write descriptively. You should not write a story.

KNOW THE EXAM

9. Judge each of the following statements in turn. Decide which ones are *true* and which are *false*:

a) In descriptive writing, you should imagine a scene in your mind and focus on it. *True* or *false*?

b) In descriptive writing, you must write a true story. *True* or *false*?

c) It is a good idea to use names in a descriptive piece. *True* or *false*?

d) You must have lots of adjectives and adverbs in your writing. *True* or *false*?

e) Brief snatches of dialogue are a good thing in descriptive writing. *True* or *false*?

f) You should definitely have all five senses in your writing. *True* or *false?*

g) You can write a descriptive piece in the first-person (*I, we*), the second-person *(you)* or the third-person *(he, she, it, they)*. *True* or *false?*

h) If there are lots of people in the your description (e.g. a crowd), it is better to generalize about them rather than pick out one or two as individuals. *True* or *false?*

Imagine the...

Now consider question B2. You have to choose one of five options available. Your task is to respond imaginatively with a piece of writing that covers about two sides of A4 paper.

The selection below is typical of the range of tasks and prompts. Two of them are straightforward titles, one is a direct instruction for personal writing, one is an 'opening line' and one is a 'last line'. The idea is genuinely that one of them will act as a stimulus for you to write a good response.

Make a considered choice, not a hurried one. Go through the process with the choices below. Which ones would you reject immediately? Which would you consider?

B2. Choose one of the following titles for your writing.

The quality of your writing is more important than its length, but as a guide think about writing between one and two sides in your answer book.

Either
a) My greatest regret.
or
b) 'And I hope I don't see them again in a hurry!' Write a story which ends with these words.
or
c) Write about an evening which you will remember for a very long time.
or

d) The Escape. Write a story with this title.

or

e) 'It was just another day on the planet Tharg when something rather unexpected happened.'
Continue this story in any way you choose.

KNOW THE EXAM

10. Again, judge each of the following statements in turn. Decide which ones are *true* and which are *false*:

a) You should start your piece of imaginative writing immediately because there is no time to waste. *True* or *false*?

b) The opening of your story is more important than the ending. *True* or *false*?

c) You should include descriptive details in a piece of imaginative writing. *True* or *false*?

d) The more you write, the better your mark will be. *True* or *false*?

e) You should restrict your story to three or four characters. *True* or *false*?

f) For most candidates, realistic stories based on personal experience work better than fictitious stories. *True* or *false*?

g) It's a good idea to change the order of the exam questions and do the imaginative writing first. *True* or *false*?

h) Examiners are prejudiced against certain kinds of stories. *True* or *false*?

THE BRAINWASH BOX

- In descriptive writing, focus on the task.

- In imaginative writing, don't show off with violence or anything else that makes you seem immature.

- Proof-read your work. You will find some errors to correct if you look properly.

Unit 6.2   Focus on ENGLISH PAPER 2

'Paper 2 is pretty much the same as Paper 1, isn't it? ... A bit of reading and a bit of writing?'

Paper 2 is different in several ways from Paper 1. It has the same structure – Section A Reading followed by Section B Writing – but it has different types of texts, questions and writing tasks.

You need to prepare properly for Paper 2, or else all your efforts on Paper 1 will be wasted.

Same but different...

Paper 2 is **the same as** Paper 1 in the following ways:

- They are both 2 hours long.
- They both have a Reading section worth 40 marks and a Writing section worth 40 marks.
- The Reading Section will contain four or five questions worth 5 or 10 marks each.
- The Writing section will contain two questions worth 20 marks each.
- In Reading, you will get credit for: finding things in the text; reading between the lines; understanding what the writer is trying to do.
- In Writing, you will be assessed for: the quality of your content and organization; the quality of your use of language.

BUT...

Paper 2 is **different from** Paper 1 in the following ways:

- There are two texts to read, not one.
- There are no line numbers down the side of the text.
- The Reading texts are media and non-fiction texts.
- The Writing tasks have very precise instructions that you are expected to follow.

Answers to the questions raised in the 'Know the Exam' boxes are in the *Teacher's Guide*.

SECTION A: READING (NON-FICTION AND MEDIA)

Remember that the two texts in this section will be media and non-fiction. One text is usually alongside the questions, while the other is often on a separate sheet, called the Resource Material. This is particularly the case if the text is a different shape or size from the normal exam paper page!

KNOW THE EXAM

1. Which of the following types of text might appear in this section of Paper 2?

   advertisements   brochures   extracts from novels   poems
   playscripts   leaflets   essays about people or topical issues
   magazine articles   newspaper reports

Reading the texts

In Paper 2 Section A, it makes sense to look at the questions right from the start. Look at the texts quickly at first. Get the correct text in front of you for the first question. Like the 'imaginary' question below, it may be a search-and-find question. You will have no help with line numbers, but you will be pointed to the relevant text. Look out for these words, or something like them:

* **Look at the newspaper article.**
  List 10 details from the text which...   **(10)**

KNOW THE EXAM

2. What important advice would you give fellow candidates for a search-and-find question?

The questions in this section are likely to include some key words that you need to feel comfortable with. In the following question, the key word is **attitude**.

An attitude is the way someone thinks, speaks or behaves about something. For example, you may have a positive attitude to your work, but you may have a carefree attitude to life in general. In the case of a writer, you need to work out what she or he believes about the topic being written about. Work out if the attitude gradually shifts or even sharply changes in the course of the piece of writing. Look out for these words, or something like them:

- **What are the writer's attitudes to...? How does the writer make these attitudes clear?**
  You should consider:
  o   **what the writer says about ...**
  o   **his/her choice of words and phrases.**

KNOW THE EXAM

3. 'Kim has had a _____attitude to studying this term.'

   Think of as many different words that could describe **attitude** in a school report like the one above. Try to find at least 10.

Media texts seek to persuade, tempt or convince...

As this section will include a media text, you will certainly be asked about the persuasive techniques of a writer. A media text may try to persuade you to buy something – a product – but it may be trying to sell you an idea: in other words, to persuade you to adopt a particular point of view. A product might be anything from a healthy breakfast cereal to a brand new car, while an idea or an argument might be a defence of fox-hunting, for example, or an attack on passive smoking.

So, expect a question in this section with the word **persuade** or **tempt** or **convince** in it. This will be a '**How...?**' question, so the focus of your answer must be on the persuasive techniques of the writer, the ways in which he or she tries to convince you that his or her way of thinking is correct. Look out for these words, or something like them:

- **Now look at the brochure.**
  How does the brochure try to tempt you to...
  You should consider:
  o   **the photograph and headline**
  o   **what the brochure says about...**
  o   **words and phrases used in the text.**

A writer may try to persuade or tempt or convince you by saying certain things, but it is **how** the things are said that make a text truly persuasive. Getting beyond 'saying' and 'telling' is vital for a successful answer. Is the writer perhaps *claiming* something ... or *promising* something ... or perhaps just quietly *suggesting* something by putting it in your mind?

Is the persuasion 'in your face' or something more subtle ... or, as in so many cases, a mixture of both?

KNOW THE EXAM

4. Think of different ways in which teachers try to persuade students to treat their work seriously. Find at least five.

'A teacher can try to persuade a student to treat his or her work seriously by _____ the student...

When you write about a media text, avoid generalized comments that could refer to any newspaper report or brochure. This is known as **vague drill** – in other words, you learn a few things about the media and drop them into your answer ... instead of making relevant comments about the text(s) on the exam paper. **Vague drill gets no marks!**

KNOW THE EXAM

5. Which of the following are useless as they stand? Which of them are probably saying something relevant to an exam answer?

a) The brochure has a big, black, bold headline.

b) The pictures in the brochure break up the text and make it more persuasive.

c) The picture of the overweight couple links with the headline.

d) The last word in the headline has a double meaning.

e) The columns are persuasive because they are in sections with sub-headings.

Read, think...and then compare

Somewhere in this section you will be asked a comparison question and you will be expected to write about both texts in the same answer. This question usually, but not always, comes as the last question of the section. The question will test your ability to make cross-references between the so-called non-fiction text and the media text. You need to be methodical and clearly organized in this answer.

Look with great care at the wording of the comparison question. Make sure you are answering the question that has been set, not one that is in your head! As with all questions in this section, read and think before you write. It is not the length of the answer that counts here, but the quality.

If you are offered bullet points in support, use them. Look out for these words, or something like them:

- **To answer this question you will need to look at both the article and the brochure.**
  Compare the ways the two texts tell you about...
  You must include comments on:
  o **who each text is aimed at**
  o **the purpose of each text**
  o **the way ... ... is presented in each text**
  o **in what ways each text would help you to...**

KNOW THE EXAM

6. What is the likely main purpose of the following types of texts?

   a) Newspaper report: to i_____ readers

   b) Advertisement: to p_____ possible customers

   c) Humorous article: to e _____ readers

   d) Argumentative article: to try to c_____ readers

   e) Review (travel, film, etc.): to a_____ readers

   f) Brochure (e.g. theme park): to t_____ possible customers

KNOW THE EXAM

7. Match each one of the **explanations** a) – e) to one of the **comparison questions** i) – v).

   a) This question invites thoughts and feelings gathered together from the two texts.

   b) This question asks clearly for comparisons as well as contrasts.

   c) This question asks you to 'weigh up' each of the texts and to make a preference.

   d) This question asks for the selection of the best bits from each of the texts.

   e) This question concentrates on the contrasts in the handling of the topic in each text.

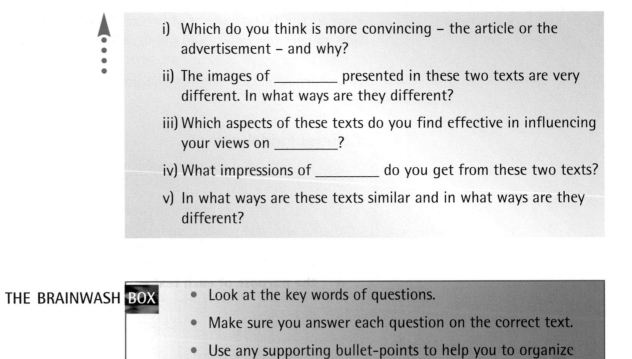

i) Which do you think is more convincing – the article or the advertisement – and why?

ii) The images of _____ presented in these two texts are very different. In what ways are they different?

iii) Which aspects of these texts do you find effective in influencing your views on _____?

iv) What impressions of _____ do you get from these two texts?

v) In what ways are these texts similar and in what ways are they different?

THE BRAINWASH BOX

- Look at the key words of questions.
- Make sure you answer each question on the correct text.
- Use any supporting bullet-points to help you to organize an answer.

SECTION B: TRANSACTIONAL AND DISCURSIVE WRITING

As in Paper 1, your writing skills will be tested in Section B. You again have to do two pieces of writing. Watch your spelling, punctuation, sentence structure and grammar at all times. Remember to use paragraphs.

Transactional writing tasks are 'real-life' writing tasks. An important part of them is their sense of **audience**. In other words, you have to direct your writing to a particular person or a range of people (sometimes narrow, sometimes wide).

Discursive tasks require you to write a reasoned **discussion** of a topic. You should try to write with enthusiasm and commitment in a way that is up-to-date and **topical**.

There is a large overlap between **transactional** and **discursive** writing tasks. Regard them as one and the same for examination purposes. In practice, the tasks will require **articles**, **letters**, **formal reports**, **leaflets/brochures** or 'speeches'.

Look at the front page of your examination paper. Remind yourself how much time you should spend on Questions B1 and B2.

Now, turn to page 4 of your examination paper. There is no choice of questions.

General guidelines

- You do not need to worry which of the tasks is transactional and which is discursive.
- The first of the two tasks will probably be linked in terms of topic or theme with the reading material in Section A. You can use the ideas from Section A, if appropriate, but do not copy chunks of the text(s).
- The second task will certainly be free-standing, i.e. not linked to any topic on the paper. Do not worry – the task will be general enough for all candidates to cope and adapt.

Write your article

B1. A teenage magazine has invited readers to write a lively article about a well known person they admire or dislike. You have decided to send in a contribution.

Write your article.

Your article could include:
- **an introduction to the person, aimed at your teenage audience**
- **the qualities you admire/dislike in this person**
- **a conclusion summing up your opinions.**

The quality of your writing is more important than its length. You should write about one to two pages in your answer book.

KNOW THE EXAM

8. Consider the task above and answer these questions:

a) What is the target audience for this particular task?

b) Give a definition and example of a suitable 'well known' person for this task.

c) Give a definition and example of someone who would not be regarded as 'well known' for this task.

> d) What general advice would you give someone writing an article that was intended to be 'lively'?
>
> e) Should the article have a headline, columns and sub-headings?

Write your letter

B2. Imagine you have a friend or relative who is considering going to live abroad.

Write a letter giving your opinions.

The quality of your writing is more important than its length, but as a guide think about writing between one and two sides in your answer book.

KNOW THE EXAM

> 9. Consider the task above and answer these questions:
>
> a) Docs the task require a formal or an informal letter?
>
> b) Think of a suitable person, destination and circumstances for the focus of this task. Give an example of a sensible choice to receive the letter.
>
> c) Should you encourage your friend to go or should you put them off going?
>
> d) Should you use selfish as well as unselfish reasons in your letter?
>
> e) Does this letter require 'Yours faithfully' or 'Yours sincerely' at the end?

Write your report

The type of transactional and discursive writing that continues to give candidates most trouble is the **formal report**.

This is NOT the same as a newspaper report. A formal report is also NOT set out as a letter. Nor is it to be confused with an end-of-year school report!

A formal report is an **official document** that a person or persons submits to an organization, about a situation of some relevance to one or both sides.

General guidelines

The report, to look at its best, requires:

- a report heading (e.g. *Report on the eating habits of school children*) and date
- the recipient of the report (e.g. *To: the Board of Governors*)
- the sender of the report (e.g. *From: a representative of the Catering Department*)
- an introduction
- sub-headings (e.g. *Main course, Dessert, Fruit and Vegetables*)
- a style that is not informal or slang
- bullet-points (a list of key points)
- conclusions/recommendations (i.e. clear suggestions for future action).

SAMPLE TASK

The Governors, who are responsible for running your school or college, are interested in the views of pupils/students.

They have asked you to write a report, pointing out what you see as the strengths and weaknesses of your school or college.

You might consider some of the following headings for your report, but feel free to choose your own:

- **Facilities and Equipment**
- **Buildings**
- **Range of Subjects**
- **Out-of-School Activities.**

Write your report for the Governors.

Guidelines:

a) Write down the heading and date for your report.

b) Write down the recipients (the receivers) of the report.

c) Write down the sender of the report.

d) Write down the opening sentence of the introduction.

e) Write down a sub-heading, different from the ones suggested in the task outline.

f) Write down three bullet-pointed recommendations.

THE BRAINWASH BOX

- Always remind yourself of the purpose of the task.

- Always remind yourself of the particular audience that you must target.

- Proof-read your work. You will find some errors to correct if you look properly.

Unit 6.3

Focus on ENGLISH LITERATURE Specification A EXAM

'As long as you know the story, you can pretty much waffle your way through a literature exam. All you need are the plot summaries for your novel and your play ...'

In an English Literature exam you do need a good knowledge of the texts you are studying, but the exam does not require you to retell the story. In fact, retelling the story is a distraction from what you should be doing – showing your understanding of characters, situations, themes, etc. Understanding means... applying your knowledge of the texts by selecting and highlighting and explaining things. Above all, understanding means... answering the question!

The English Literature exam is $2\frac{1}{2}$ hours long, probably the longest 'desk-bound' exam in your experience.

Answers to the questions raised in the 'Know the Exam' boxes are in the *Teacher's Guide*.

KNOW THE EXAM

1. How long should you spend on:

Section A?   Section B?   Section C?

The exam paper itself may also be the thickest – but don't be alarmed. There will be questions on eight prose texts (Section A) and eight drama texts (Section B), as listed on the front cover, but you only have to write on one of each! You also, of course, must write about the 'unseen' poem in Section C.

Below is a typical set of questions on a set text. You must answer question (a) based on an extract (printed on the facing page of the exam paper). Then you must choose an essay question, either question (b) or question (c).

The extract question is worth a total of 10 marks; the essay question is worth 20 marks.

Sample questions on a set text

Answer part (a) and **either** part (b) or part (c).

You are advised to spend about 20 minutes on part (a), and about 40 minutes on part (b) or part (c).

(a) Read the extract on the opposite page. Then answer the following questions:

(i) What do you think of the way _____ speaks and behaves here? (5)

(ii) Choose parts of the extract that you find particularly effective. Write about them, explaining why you find them effective. (5)

Either

(b) What do you think of _____?

Think about:
- the way the author describes him/her and his/her way of life
- his/her relationships with...
- the incident with...
- the way s/he speaks and behaves. (20)

Or

(c) Imagine you are _____. At the end of the story you think back over what has happened. Write down your thoughts and feelings.

You may wish to think about:
- your attitudes to...
- your relationships with...
- your feelings about... (20)

KNOW THE EXAM

2. Look at the sample questions on page 153.

  a) Do you think it would be OK to write one answer to cover the two parts of the extract question?

  b) Do you think you should aim for half a side or a side of an exam booklet for your answer to an extract question?

  c) What are the differences between question (b) and question (c) in this particular sample set of questions?

  d) What length of answer do you think you should target for question (b) or (c)?

Extract questions

You should track through the extract and annotate it. This means you should systematically follow the text and underline key words and phrases.

Then write your answer. Start by briefly explaining why the extract is important in the story. Try to sum up what you intend to say in the rest of your answer. Then comment on particular details that you find interesting. Remember that you should only take 20 minutes for an extract question.

KNOW THE EXAM

3. Why do you think comments are more important than quotations in answers to extract questions?

Essay (and empathy) questions

You may have the choice of two essay questions or you may have one essay question and one empathy task to choose from.

Essay questions can be asked about characters, relationships, themes, openings and endings. Some of the questions on characters may be empathy tasks in which you pretend you are a specific character and have to try to write in the 'voice' of the character.

In any essay there is a danger of waffle. Remember that everything you say has to be rooted in the text. Always focus on the question in your introduction, and sum up what you've said in your conclusion. Try to show the examiner how well you know the whole text, so even if the question is on a specific part, make it clear that you know what happens elsewhere.

You are not expected to learn lots of quotations for essays. In fact, you can get trapped into quoting aimlessly just because you have memorized part of the text. This is not sensible!

You can show your detailed knowledge of the text by using names confidently, referring directly to specific details, paraphrasing and using very short, embedded quotations.

KNOW THE EXAM

4. Essay and empathy questions

   a) How can you successfully 'write in the voice of the character' in an empathy task?

   b) What is paraphrasing?

   c) What is an embedded quotation?

Use the right words

Section A and Section B of the English Literature exam deal with 'long' texts, and there is a common language of 'story'. There are routine 'technical' words that novels and plays share, but there are also words that apply to one and not the other. You send a poor signal to the examiner, for example, if you refer to your novel as a play, or vice-versa.

KNOW THE EXAM

5.

Differences between prose and drama texts

a) Prose has **readers**. It also has **descriptions** and **paragraphs** and **chapters**.

   Think of 'technical' words that you can use when writing specifically about a drama text, e.g. *actor*. Make a list of at least six words.

Similarities between prose and drama texts

b) Now think of 'technical' words that you can use when writing about either prose or drama, e.g. *narrator*. Make a list of at least six words.

The 'unseen' poem

Leave a good 30 minutes at the end of the exam for the 'unseen' poem in Section C. 'Unseen' means that you are not expected to have read the poem ever before, so you must use five minutes at least to unlock its meaning. You will need to read it at least twice and annotate it in some detail, before writing your response.

General guidelines

- Use the same technique as with the prose and drama extracts – work out an overall position, then track through, focusing on detail as closely as possible.

- You are not expected to 'know the answer'. You can use words like 'perhaps' and 'maybe' to establish your caution and your thoughtfulness.

- Try to comment on style – the way the poet writes the poem – but don't worry too much about knowing the correct terms. What the examiner really wants to see is that you can look at how the poem works.

- Look also at the poem's structure – the length of lines and stanzas (verses), the way the poem looks on the page.

- Be confident enough to give a personal response – if you are a reasonably sensitive person, your views will be valued.

- Always use the title – it may give you a way in to discussing the poem.

Sample question on an 'unseen' poem

Write about the poem and its effect on you.

You may wish to include some or all of these points:
- the poem's content – what it is about
- the ideas the poet may have wanted us to think about
- the mood or atmosphere of the poem
- how it is written – words or phrases you find interesting, the way the poem is structured or organized, and so on
- your response to the poem.

KNOW THE EXAM

6. Decide if each of the following sentences would be worth a tick from an examiner. Judge each one as *yes* or *no*.

a) The title of the poem is 'Hurricane', which tells us that the poem is going to be about a hurricane.

b) The title indicates literally the subject of this poem.

c) The poem leaves you with a sad feeling.

d) On the last line the poet says '...............'.

e) The poet uses lots of similes and metaphors.

f) The weather in this poem is a pathetic fallacy.

THE BRAINWASH BOX

- Always answer the question – don't waffle.

- In extract questions and in the 'unseen' poem, track the text patiently and selectively.

- Be wary of technical language – don't use words you don't fully understand.

Unit 6.4

Focus on ENGLISH LITERATURE Specification B EXAM

'Great! I'm in the B team. It shouldn't be too hard ...'

There are no shortcuts to success in Specification B. Although the exam is organized differently, you are still expected to be able to write about texts in detail (extract questions) and also to be able to discuss whole texts (referring to overall ideas, especially in essay questions). The standard required by the WJEC at each grade is the same for Specification B as for Specification A.

What makes the Specification B exam different?

- The set novel and the 'unseen' poem of Specification A are replaced by the 50-page WJEC Anthology of prose extracts, short stories and poems.
- Candidates will be presented with a 'clean' copy of the Anthology at the start of the Specification B exam for use during the exam.
- Comparison of texts is a key feature of Specification B. (In Specification A, comparison is covered in coursework.)

What are the similarities between Specification A and B exams?

- They are both $2\frac{1}{2}$ hours long.
- They both have three sections.
- They both include prose, poetry and drama.
- The skills tested are almost entirely the same.

Summary of the Specification B exam

- Section A: Prose Anthology – extract question, followed by a choice of essay questions.
- Section B: Poetry Anthology – extract question, followed by a choice of essay questions.
- Section C: Drama set text – choice of essay questions.

Answers to the questions raised in the 'Know the Exam' box are in the *Teacher's Guide*.

KNOW THE EXAM

1. How long are you expected to spend on:
   Section A?   Section B?   Section C?

2. In each of sections A and B, how long are you expected to spend on:
   the extract question?   the comparison question?

3. How many marks is each of the extract questions worth?
4. How many marks is each comparison question worth?
5. How many marks is the Drama essay section worth?

THE BRAINWASH BOX

- Always answer the question – don't waffle.

- In extract questions, track the text patiently and selectively.

- In comparison (essay) questions, deal with the two texts reasonably equally.

Unit 6.5

The bottom line

'I wasn't listening ... what was it you said?'

During the GCSE course

- **Treat every lesson as a Speaking and Listening lesson.**
  Take part – communicate clearly – be silent when necessary.

- **Keep coursework under control.**
  Be sensible with the length (not shorter than three sides of A4, but not longer than six sides).
  Be honest ('all your own work').
  Take your teacher's general advice, but don't expect detailed corrections.
  Be on time with every piece.

Before the GCSE exams

- **Revise by using past papers in both English and English Literature.**
  Practise by writing answers of the length required in the exam, then by answering 'against the clock'.
  Read as many WJEC question papers as you can, even if you don't attempt to write answers for all of them.

In the GCSE exams

- **Use the full amount of time in each exam. Divide the time correctly for the individual questions.**
  Look at the key words in each question. Before you start to write down a response to any question, organize your answer quickly in your head.

Well, that's all sorted then ... Good luck!